TURTON WORKHOUSE

David J Leeming

Publication No 34   November 2011

No 34 Turton Workhouse
David J Leeming
Published by Turton Local History Society November 2011
ISBN 978-1-904974 34-5

TURTON LOCAL HISTORY SOCIETY

Turton Local History Society exists to promote an interest in history by discussion, research and record. It is particularly concerned with the history of the old Urban District of Turton, Lancashire and its constituent ancient townships of Bradshaw, Edgworth, Entwistle, Harwood, Longworth, Quarlton and Turton.

Previous publications of Turton Local History Society are listed on the inside front cover.

Meetings of the Society will be held at 7.30pm on the fourth Wednesday of each month (except for June, July August and December) at Longsight Methodist Church Hall, Harwood. Visitors are welcome.

ACKNOWLEDGEMENTS

Sincere thanks are due to the many people who have helped by sharing their knowledge, memories, documents and notes, all of which have made this publication possible.

The author is especially indebted to the late Helen Heyes who provided much well researched material that gave a sound basis from which to complete this work.

Thanks are also due to the late Jim Francis who gave some sound advice in the early stages of compilation and to Eileen Cowen for the photograph of Lancaster Asylum.

The staff of Bolton Archives, Lancashire Record Office and The Bolton News are to be thanked for their help, the use of reports and the provision of photographs.

CONTENTS

Page

Chapter 1		THE POOR LAW	
	1.1	Origins	1
	1.2	The Sixteenth Century	2
	1.3	The Poor Law Act of 1601	5
	1.4	The Poor Law Act of 1834	7
	1.5	The Workhouse	9
	1.6	End of the Workhouse System	12
Chapter 2		THE POOR LAW IN BOLTON PARISH	
	2.1	Early Provisions	15
	2.2	Effects of the 1834 Act	16
	2.3	Connections between local Workhouses	20
Chapter 3		THE POOR LAW IN TURTON c1730-1829	
	3.1	The Townships	23
	3.2	The Chetham Charity	25
	3.3	The Nineteenth Century	27
Chapter 4		ACTIVE YEARS AT TURTON 1830-1861	
	4.1	The 1830s	35
	4.2	The 1840s	37
	4.3	The 1850s	43
	4.4	Food, meals and diet	43
	4.5	The Farm	46
	4.6	Education	48
	4.7	Accommodation	50
	4.8	Health and medical matters	53
	4.9	Religion	55
	4.10	Equipment	56
	4.11	Ongoing problems	56
Chapter 5		CLOSURE, PUBLIC HOUSE AND DEMOLITION	
	5.1	Closure and sale	60
	5.2	The Beerhouse	64
APPENDIX 1		TRUSTEES AND GOVERNORS	70
APPENDIX 2		MAINTENANCE, BAPTISMS AND BURIALS	71
APPENDIX 3		CENSUS RETURNS	74

ILLUSTRATIONS

	Page
Artist's impression of Turton Workhouse.	front cover
OS map showing Turton Workhouse in 1848.	title page
Street whipping in Tudor times.	4
Street begging in Tudor times.	4
Mealtime for male workhouse inmates.	11
Mealtime for female workhouse inmates.	11
OS 25 inch map of 1910 showing Bolton Poor Law Offices.	14
OS 6 inch map of 1847 showing Fletcher Street workhouse in Bolton.	17
Plaque at the site of Brindle Workhouse.	21
Riot at Stockport Workhouse in 1842.	21
Doffcocker Inn, formerly the Halliwell Workhouse.	22
Lancaster Moor Asylum.	22
The former Entwistle Workhouse.	24
The former Harwood Workhouse.	24
Order for cloth for a pauper child.	27
Letting notice for Goose Cote Hill Farm.	30
Receipt for cloth bought for the poor.	30
Bolton Methodist preachers' plan of 1818.	31
List of cloth lengths distributed to poor people, 1819.	33
Letter from the Workhouse Master and plan of proposed alterations.	34
Map of the 'Bolton Union'.	36
Admission form for entrants to Turton Workhouse.	38
OS 6 inch map of 1848 showing Turton Workhouse and adjacent area.	41
Notice of Public Vestry Meeting in 1849.	41
Cox Green Road in 1939.	42
Cox Green Road in 1910.	42
Plan of Goose Cote Farm.	47
Plan of the old hospital at Goose Cote.	47
Receiving Order for admission to Prestwich Asylum.	57
Statement Form for admission to Prestwich Asylum.	58
Notice for letting Goose Cote Hill Farm.	59
The Sportsman's Arms Inn.	59
Notices of sale and auction of the former workhouse.	61
Map showing the Bolton Union Workhouse at Fishpool in 1891.	62
The Bolton Union Workhouse at Fishpool when new.	62
Notice for the sale of the De Rothwell Arms in 1891.	64
The De Rothwell Arms c1910.	65
Plan of the De Rothwell Arms.	66
Cox Green Quarry and the former workhouse c1920.	66
Advertisement for Alexandra Brewery.	67
Map showing De Rothwell Cottages and Cox Green Quarry in 1890s.	68
Turton UDC Committee inspecting at Cox Green Quarry in 1946.	68
Site of the former Turton Workhouse in 2011.	69
Cox Green Road adjacent to the quarry.	69
Walmsley Chapel.	73
Rules to be observed at Turton Workhouse	inner back cover
Former Poor Law Offices in Mawdsley Street, Bolton	outer back cover

CHAPTER I   THE POOR LAW

1.1   Origins

From Anglo-Saxon times laws have existed to cover the needs of the poor, aged and infirm. Poverty often haunted peoples' lives when lack of food reserves and scant means of transport outside established villages and towns often brought local communities into dire need.

As early as AD 928 King Athelstan the Glorious, who boasted he was the first monarch of all England, ordained that if any landless man should settle in another shire and seek his kinsfolk; the kinsfolk may harbour him on condition that they make compensation for him.

Under King Canute (AD 1017-1035) everyone had to be brought into a Hundred and in it held in surety. Each householder was held responsible for the individuals of his household, whether bond or free, and for any stranger he had admitted under his roof. These early feudal laws had the effect of restraining and repressing vagrants by not allowing them any maintenance. Feudalism, a system of holding land from a superior in return for service, tended to depress the many and elevate the few, increasing the difference between the social classes.

The reign of Edward 1 (Longshanks) saw a determination to enforce the law. In 1285 the Statute of Winchester made each hundred responsible for all robberies within its limits and required that the gates of walled towns be closed between sunset and sunrise. Anyone who witnessed a crime had to play a part in pursuing the criminal until he was apprehended. The suburbs were to be searched for undesirables and every man was held responsible for lodgers in his house.

Monasticism played an important part in the life of mediaeval Lancashire and elsewhere. The first local monastery was founded at Lancaster in 1094 and others followed in the 12th and 13th centuries. Only three were ever of any size: the Austin Canons of Cockersand and the Cistercian abbeys of Furness and Whalley. Monasteries and convents gave succour to the poor and needy as part of their Christian duty, and the Church with its schools, hospitals and pious laity did what it could to relieve physical distress and provide comfort to those in need.

The marked reduction in population and shortage of labour caused by the Black Death in 1348 made life less local and resulted in greater movement of people between towns. Problems of vagrancy increased for the authorities as people began to seek work or charity outside their own neighbourhoods. Efforts to reduce vagrancy were made by whipping and by hanging for repeated offences, but this did little to reduce the number of vagrants.

In 1349, in Edward III's reign, no alms were to be given to any person fit for labour. At the close of his reign the House of Commons was complaining that servants and labourers were quitting their service at the slightest causes, some leading a wild life in towns, others wandering in parties around the country becoming beggars and robbers. The decay of the old feudal system brought about a new aspect of poverty and an increasing vagrancy. Many who had struggled for freedom had to resort to begging whenever employment or other means of livelihood was not obtainable.

Two statutes of Edward III concerned artificers and servants: *'no servant or labourer, man or woman, shall depart at the end of his term, out of the Hundred or similar area where he is dwelling, to serve or dwell elsewhere or go on pilgrimage, unless he bring a letter patent containing the cause of his going, under the king's seal; and if any servant or labourer be found in any city or borough or elsewhere wandering without such letter, he shall be taken and put in the stocks, and kept there until he hath found surety to return to his service, or to serve and labour in the town from whence he came.'* None were to receive such persons without a testimonial and servants, artificers and apprentices *'shall be compelled to serve in harvest to gather and bring in the corn.'* Wages were fixed and servants and labourers were prohibited from wandering.

During the reign of Richard II (1377-1399) persons who had been in bondage were becoming more determined to be free and evade bond labour. The state intervened to make good shortcomings in the law in 1388 and 1391 by consolidating restrictions on movement and directing that a proportion of a parish's tithes, when available, were to be used for the relief of poverty. This reign is considered by some historians to be the origin of the English Poor Law.

1.2   The Sixteenth Century

In the 16th century the Tudors were the first to face the problems of poverty and vagrancy with any determination and experiment with an administration to control them. From the 12th to the early 16th centuries, the monks controlled large estates, but the dissolution of the monasteries in the 1530s caused the Church's efforts to largely cease, although around one third of the population lived in poverty. Bad harvests resulted in lack of food, high prices, and no work. Alms houses, mainly run by Christian charities, had existed from the middle ages, but were no longer able to cope with the needs of the many poor. In 1536 an Act was passed to provide relief for the needy. In 1550 another Act made every parish responsible for building a poorhouse and local clergy were authorized to ask wealthy parishioners to provide money for its building and subsequent maintenance.

The Tudors maintained a distinction between the aged, the poor, the impotent and those who were able-bodied. The principle adopted was that the parish should take responsibility for its own needy by providing outdoor relief in the form of assistance with money, food, clothing, and other goods. This relief was doled out to individuals and families in temporary distress, who had been born or lived for three years in the same precinct (township or parish), so that they were not compelled to resort to openly begging. Those not qualified for relief were given licenses by the justices to beg within certain areas, according to their means. Anyone begging outside of their precincts or without a license was whipped or set in stocks for three days and nights with only bread and water.

Until 1572 a series of experimental Acts were made to control vagrants and beggars. Able bodied vagrants found wandering, begging and unable to account for how they got their living, were punished by whipping and sworn to return to the place where they were born or had dwelt within the last three years and there put to continual labour. No money was to be given in alms but only to the common boxes and common gatherings of the parish, upon pain of forfeiture of ten times as much as was given. A book provided by the parish giving lists of the aged, poor and impotent was to be kept by the justices and other officers. Although changes and modifications were made to the above Acts the system proved largely unsuccessful and charity was eventually abandoned as a source of funds for the relief of poverty.

In 1572 previous Acts were repealed and the first legislation for a compulsory poor rate was passed. The rate was imposed at local level and made alleviation of poverty a matter for each parish. Churchwardens and overseers of the poor were appointed to provide work, apprentice pauper children, and provide for the needy. From 1576 each parish had to store wool, hemp, flax and iron so the poor could be set to work.

All above the age of 14, deemed to be sturdy beggars, rogues, or vagrants and caught begging, wandering or misbehaving were brought before one of the justices and taken to the common gaol. Harsh punishments such as whipping in a public place on market day were handed out to both men and women. Offenders, if considered to be felons, were '*grievously whipped and bored through the gristle of the right ear with a hot iron to the compass of an inch about*'. Persistent offenders were hanged. An honest householder could, if willing, take such offender into his own service for one complete year and enter into a bond with the justices to pay £5 should the offender abscond. Offenders had to appear at the Sessions at the year end. If death had occurred, the householder was liable to pay 12d. If the offender absconded and was retaken he was punished as aforesaid. Anyone found harbouring such rogues or vagrants and not having

Street whipping in Tudor times.

Begging in the street.

a licence from the justices was fined not more than £1. The term *'rogues and vagrants'* included those using craft and unlawful games or plays, card sharps, gypsies, fortune tellers, fencers (sword users), bearwards (keepers of bears used for entertainment), common players in interludes and minstrels, pedlars, tinkers, petty chapmen, counterfeiters, freed convicts, and common labourers refusing to work.

A record was retained of all the poor, aged and impotent settled in their parishes by the justices. All inhabitants were levied to *'such charges as they and every one of them shall weekly contribute towards the relief of the said poor'*. Collectors (church sidesmen) were appointed and the money delivered to the poor. Overseers, elected from the more substantial householders, kept accounts of the proceedings and presented them at regular intervals to the justices for signature. Overseers were appointed for one year, or fined 10 shillings if they refused. If any collectors refused to serve they were fined 40 shillings and the money put to the use of the poor. Inhabitants refusing to pay towards the poor were brought before two justices and committed to gaol if they persisted. Poor children below 14 and above 5 years of age that lived idle lives, or were caught begging, could be put to service by any willing householder. Boys were bound to the age of 24 and girls to 18. Mothers and fathers of bastards were to pay maintenance money weekly towards the sustenance of their child – if they failed they were committed to gaol. No one was to willingly or knowingly convey a vagrant or rogue from Ireland or the Isle of Man; any such were immediately transported back. Notwithstanding the foregoing, it is generally agreed by historians that nothing much was achieved to relieve the poor until the Elizabethan Act of 1601.

1.3 The Poor Law Act 1601

The 1601 Poor Law Act consolidated the results of the earlier experiments and built a framework of poor law administration for the next 300 years. This provision of a safety net for social failures became known as 'The Great Poor Law'. Rather than being one particular Act, the Poor Law was based on the 1601 Act but eventually comprised a whole series of Acts and local by-laws passed at different times between 1601 and 1834. The major features were the continuing concerns for the poor, impotent and aged and implementation of the rules of settlement, and outdoor relief.

The laws of settlement attempted to provide some check on mobility, but, failing this, they ensured that at least one parish was responsible for anyone born in England or Wales. If in doubt, a persons applying for relief could always be removed to their place of birth and that parish would be responsible for relief.

Every Easter, under the supervision of the justices, each parish and township appointed overseers to help the churchwardens collect the poor rate and take charge of the poor. Overseers and churchwardens had the duty of assessing the poor rate, granting outdoor relief and, at the end of their term, making a true and perfect account to the justices. Parish or township constables, appointed each year from among the householders, played their part by bringing vagrants before the justices, having them publicly whipped and then dispatching them on their painful and unhappy journey from constable to constable until they reached the place legally responsible for them.

The first 'workhouse', recorded in 1652, provided very basic shelter, food and clothing for the inmates who performed menial and monotonous tasks to earn their keep. Justices were ordered to erect Houses of Correction to provide shelter for vagrants, beggars, those unwilling to work and petty offenders. They were structurally designed for the punishment and correction of inmates. A *'Pauper Indentured Apprenticeship Certificate'* was introduced and money provided from the rates to train pauper children, under a master or mistress, in a job where they would no longer be a burden on the public.

Social and economic changes after the Civil War affected nearly all classes of society and caused many parishes to be faced with a much larger number of poor persons than ever before. The 1662 Act of Settlement established to which parish a person belonged and allowed an officer to forbid a labourer from moving into a parish if it was feared that he might someday become a burden on its poor rate. Parish officers were also to remove strangers within 40 days of arrival, unless the newcomers occupied property worth £10 per year rentable value, a prohibitive sum for many. One effect was to make it difficult for people to find work outside their own parish, hence, an amending Act of 1697, permitted officers to issue a *'Settlement Certificate'* to anyone who wanted to travel to look for employment elsewhere. The certificate carried a parish promise to accept the person named and provide for him or her should it become necessary. The Act revived the practice of *'badging the poor'* on the shoulder with a prominent letter P followed by the initial letter of the responsible parish.

By the end of the 18th century the 1782 Gilbert's Act had established poor houses for the aged and infirm. In rural southern England the Speenhamland System of outdoor relief to the poor was set up in 1795. This was started by the local magistrates in the Berkshire village of Speenhamland who felt that the Poor Law, in its current state, required more assistance than had generally been given. A series of bad harvests caused a shortage of wheat resulting in a sharp rise in the price of bread. The situation was aggravated by the increasing population and the effects of the French Wars (1793-1815) that prevented the import of grain from Europe. Things were so bad that famine was a distinct possibility and there was a fear among the ruling classes that the lower orders might be tempted to emulate the French and revolt. Relief was given according to the price of bread and the number of children in a family. Every *'poor and industrious person'* received a sum of money each week in addition to his wages, so much for himself and so much for members of his family. As the price of a loaf rose, the dole was to rise with it. Although this system was widely used in the south of the country, the northern counties were largely unaffected. It did not establish itself in Lancashire where there was often a general labour shortage in the factories and mines and agricultural wages were adequate.

The basic 1601 legislation was adequate for the rural population at that time, but during the latter part of the 18th century, the population increased enormously and massive social changes occurred as the largely rural economy changed to one based on industry. During the Industrial Revolution masses of people gathered into small areas causing overcrowding, poverty and destitution. Even though the economy was gaining strength, there were cycles of industrial depression that led to temporary unemployment and hardship in many industrial areas.

1.4   The Poor Law of 1834

Social unrest during and following the French Wars and a rise in the cost of poor relief, led to the appointment of a Royal Commission in 1832 and a review of the Poor Law. The main recommendations were incorporated in the 1834 Poor Law Amendment Act (sometimes known as the New Poor Law) which completely altered the existing legislation. Under the new Act parishes were grouped into administrative units called '*Unions*'. To manage each Union, Guardians were elected by open ballot of ratepayers and property owners in each parish, together with representatives from each constituent parish and some ex-officio members. Justices of the Peace became ex-officio guardians. The activities of the Boards of Guardians were subject to supervision by a Poor Law Commission; although in practice they retained considerable autonomy.

The administration was controlled centrally by the Poor Law Commissioners based at Somerset House, London, with Assistant Commissioners acting as their agents throughout the country. The Poor Law Commission sat from 1834 to 1847.

The initial Commission was for 5 years with annual reviews until 1842 and then for a further 5 years. The Assistant Commissioners organized the division of England and Wales into Poor Law Unions and implemented instructions from London. Each Assistant Commissioner was responsible for a particular district, often covering large parts of a county. The Assistant Commissioners possessed definite administrative powers but these became curtailed under a new 'Poor Law Board', which lasted from 1847 to 1871.

Although the *'Unions'* replaced the parish system almost immediately in some areas, poor relief continued to be administered with little change in others. Some authorities waited until agitation had died down before giving relief under the 1834 Act, which was primarily intended to help the agricultural south and east where pauperism had become a way of life. It was less relevant in Lancashire where industrial employment was available for most people, most of the time.

In general, the Poor Law Commissioners and later the Poor Law Board Inspectors encouraged the Guardians to apply a rigid outdoor labour test to all able-bodied applicants for relief, and the test was made compulsory under an order of 1842. The terms of the test were devised to be particularly irksome so that the erection and operation of a workhouse would become a preferred option for the Guardians. But in the northern industrial areas they were loath to apply the test to cotton operatives and others thrown out of work in cyclical trade depressions. If such operatives, conditioned to fairly dexterous work in a warm mill, were given heavy manual work such as stone-breaking, it was recognised that their health and their hands might be ruined. If they were to be tested in their own work, huge factories would be needed - an obvious impossibility. Therefore in the northern areas, the outdoor labour test was reserved for paupers, vagrants, and idlers.

Opposition to the new Poor Law was most pronounced in industrial towns, where it was not only thought to be an attack on the living standards of the working man and his family, but an attempt to punish and treat as criminals those who, through no fault of their own, were unemployed or earning low wages. In the industrial depressions which affected northern towns from time to time, workers could quickly lose their employment. Both employers and employees in the textile and other industries preferred liberal outdoor relief at slack times and for the workhouses and almshouses to be reserved for the aged and impotent. Generally, the employer wanted outdoor relief to hold his workforce together, whilst the employees regarded such outdoor relief as their right, as a return for their contributions to the nation's wealth. Local opposition in the Bolton Union delayed the election of Guardians and transfer of responsibility of relief to them until 1839.

1.5　The Workhouse

Each Union usually had a central workhouse to provide indoor relief, with responsibility for day-to-day management in the hands of a master and his wife. If needed, further assistance was provided by a number of paid officers. The construction of a workhouse was financed partly by the local Poor Law Rates and partly through government loans that had to be repaid. Running costs were met by local rates, but income could also be generated from the work of inmates.

It has been argued that the workhouse system was the first attempt at social welfare in this country and laid the foundations of the modern welfare state. In this respect it was 100 years ahead of its time, yet implementation of the high ideals of the reformers and legislators responsible for the New Poor Law went tragically wrong and the workhouse became a dreaded place of shame, suffering and despair. They were purposely made repellent to encourage the able-bodied to maintain themselves and their families outside for as long as possible. Some people would rather have died than go there - and some did!

Each post-1834 purpose built workhouse was designed to accommodate several hundred people, the aim being that *'the poor shall be set to work, and shall dwell in working houses'*. The 1834 Act proposed separate workhouses with internal divisions for different categories of paupers, but within a year or two, economy and ease of management dictated that mixed workhouses became the norm. These were built to house the old, the sick, the chronically infirm, children, and the mentally disabled, as well as unemployed able-bodied men and women. One of the great scandals of the workhouse was the condition of the insane who mingled with the sane. The average cost of a lunatic in a workhouse was 3s per week, but in an asylum the cost was 9s or more and some Boards of Guardians had to be compelled by the Lunacy Commissioners to remove lunatics to asylums or even to separate them from the workhouse children. In some Unions an insane pauper might share a bed with 2 sane paupers. Such a great diversity of people under one roof was doomed to failure.

So that the workhouse should be a *'place of last resort'* a rigid inflexible system of discipline and punishment was introduced. Families were separated, men from women, husbands from wives, brothers from sisters and children over seven were taken away from their mothers. The official policy was that children and babies below 7 could stay with their mothers in women's quarters, otherwise families would be split up on entry and sent to different buildings, where they would be confined till they met again outside the gates, often penniless and homeless.

Radical reformers considered the *'workhouse labour test'* to be the most monstrous feature of the New Poor Law. The test was hated in the industrial areas where workhouses were called *'poor law bastilles'*. Opponents of the system thought that workhouses ought to be places of retreat where poor men and women were free to intermingle, and enter or leave at any time. Attempts at stricter supervision were regarded as interference with personal liberty

The 1834 Act required three hours a day of elementary education (basic numeracy and literacy) for children, and a schoolmaster was employed by each Board of Guardians. When the Education Act of 1870 was passed, children were removed from mixed workhouses, placed in separate establishments and sent to the local Board School. Under the 1834 Act a qualified medical officer was required to attend the sick, but nursing was often carried out by untrained female inmates. In workhouses, where large groups of people were confined, infectious diseases spread like wildfire and TB was rife.

After 1850 workhouse inmates were in the main the old, the sick, the handicapped, children and unmarried mothers. The stigma of illegitimacy destroyed the lives of millions of unfortunate young women and blighted those of their children. If a girl's lover deserted her and her parents could not, or would not, support her and the child, the workhouse was often the only form of relief available. The baby would be born in the workhouse infirmary. After weaning, the mother would be encouraged to leave the workhouse with her baby to seek employment. But this was usually impossible because of the limited labour market for women, further restricted because of the baby. The mother would also be encouraged to give her baby up for adoption. Many mothers were medically certified as *'hysterical'* or *'of unsound mind'* or even *'morally degenerate'*, and their babies forcibly removed and brought up in the workhouse. The young mother would be expected to leave the workhouse, find work outside, and contribute to the poor rates to offset the cost of keeping and educating her child. If she could not find work, she would have to return to the women's section of the workhouse. The system was heartless and stupid, but the rules reflected the social attitude that a *'fallen woman'* should be punished.

Work in a workhouse was usually boring and strenuous. Males were expected to dig, cut wood, grind corn and break-up stones for road making. The size of the crushed stones was determined by passing them through holes in an iron grille. Females did the mundane chores of cleaning, washing, scrubbing and needlework.

For punishment, some were employed on oakum picking which consisted of unraveling lengths of rope and teasing out the fibres to mix with tar for sealing wooden ships. On entry, vagrants were given a hot bath and clean clothes while their own clothes were fumigated; then a hammock, metal bed frame or woodenplank for sleeping on. In general, internal discipline in the new workhouses was stricter and the inmates lost their

Mealtime for male inmates at a London workhouse c 1900.

Mealtime for women at Mitcham Workhouse, Surrey in 1896.

freedom to enter and leave when they wanted, but medical attention and cleanliness was better, inmates' clothes were cleaner and paid officers were available to care for the sick and infirm.

Registers of local poor law officials were compiled which included the workhouse master, matron, chaplain, relieving officer, medical officer, teacher, porter (and more besides in larger institutions). One reason for keeping registers was to prevent officers dismissed for corruption from gaining employment in other workhouses. The registers included full names of paid officials, dates of their service, and the reason for resignation annotated in red. They also contained notes of various allowances granted to each official, such as for rations.

The Poor Law Certified School Act 1862 permitted Boards of Guardians to send children to special institutions such as for the blind, deaf and dumb. 1870 saw the commencement of boarding pauper children with foster parents and training apprenticeships for boys were introduced. Provision was made for casual wards for vagrants in 1871. In 1879 powers were given to the Boards of Guardians to subscribe to voluntary hospitals (such as Bolton Royal Infirmary), nursing associations, and institutions likely to render aid to persons in receipt of Poor Law relief. A Local Government Board initiative in 1886 encouraged the setting up of work relief projects when unemployment was high. 1889 brought powers to Guardians to take children from the control of parents who were unfit to look after them, by reason of vicious habits or unsatisfactory life style, or who had deserted them.

In terms of public acceptance, the setting up of Unions and Boards of Guardians to administer workhouses was doomed to failure from the start, and for some time thousands of workers in rural and some urban areas were faced with the alternatives of struggling on in abject poverty, or entering the inhuman workhouse. Eventually the national economy and working conditions did improve, albeit slowly. Better wages were eventually paid and working class families gradually acquired a pride in independence and loathing of the workhouse and relief.

1.6 End of the Workhouse System

By 1890 further extensive improvements to Poor Law infirmaries were in hand following increasing specialisation in medicine. In 1905 the government set up a Royal Commission on the Poor Law. The 1908 Old Age Pension Act followed which resulted in an allowance being given to the aged poor to live in their own homes. Half a million people became eligible to receive 5 shillings a week each or 7s 6d for a married couple.

The 1909 Royal Commission on Health and Social Change found an overwhelming need to change both the law and public attitudes towards poverty. Following a controversial report proposing the abolition of the stigma of pauperism and penury associated with the Poor Law and its workhouses, it recommended that:

1   Workhouses as then constituted, should give place to specialised institutions for the sick, the aged-poor, the young and the mentally feeble. From 1913 the term *'Workhouse'* was to be replaced by *'Poor Law Institution'*.

2.   Boards of Guardians were to be replaced by local authority Public Assistance Committees, with co-opted members.

3.   There should be separate regimes for the aged and weak, the able-bodied unemployed and the 'loafers'.

4   Vagrants and shirkers should be sent to detention colonies: i.e. Australia, or Canada. [The reaction of the 'colonies' is not recorded.]

5   A national system of labour exchanges should be set up to help the unemployed find work and improve the mobility of the workforce.

Instead of *'The Union'*, a new administration was proposed for each county or county borough, Boards of Guardians were to be replaced by Public Assistance Authorities. New Public Assistance Committees were to be appointed for dealing with applications for relief. Councils of Voluntary Aid, and various sub-committees were to organise the charities of an area under a Charity Commission. Public assistance and private charity functions were to be co-ordinated.

The Public Assistance Authority was to be a statutory committee of each County or County Borough, half of the members were to belong to the local council, and half were to be co-opted from outside; these to be nominated by Urban and Rural District Councils. The status of senior Local Government Officers was to be raised, with much greater care taken in the selection of officials. The salaries were to be adequate to attract men with powers of organisation and high moral qualities.

No children were to be left in the workhouse, even when these became 'institutions' and renewed supervision was to be exercised over children on outdoor relief.

Boards of Guardians were finally abolished and Poor Law administration transferred to county and county borough councils in 1929. The National Assistance Act, 1948 destroyed what remained of the traditional poor law policy. The National Assistance Board and the Local Authorities assisted persons in need. The 1948 Act also made further provision for the welfare of the disabled, sick, and aged, amended the law relating to non-contributory Old Age Pensions and made provision for burial or cremation of the deceased.

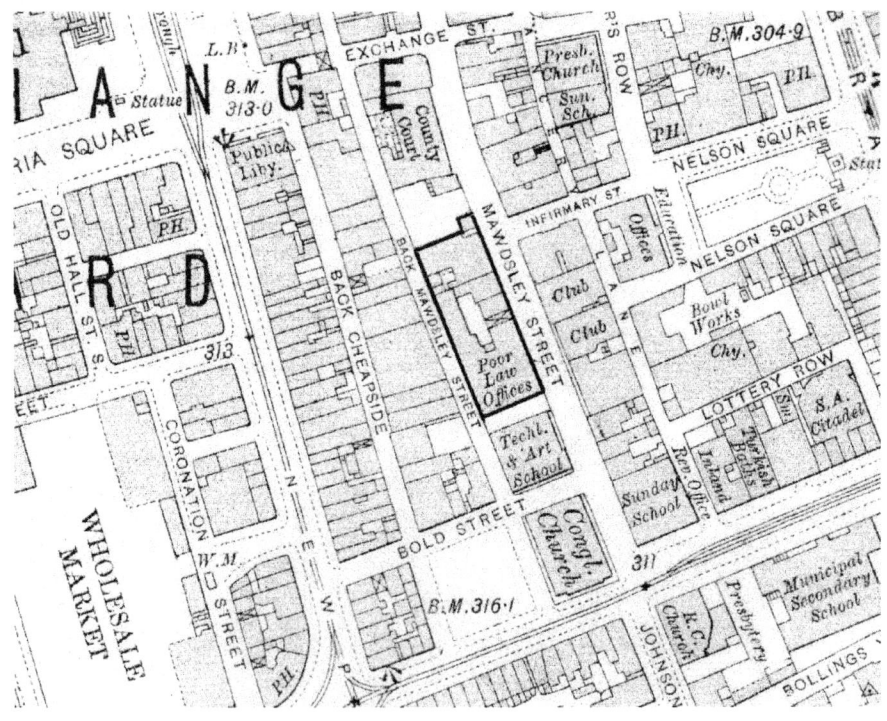

1910 25 inch OS Map showing Bolton Poor Law Offices in Mawdsley Street.

CHAPTER II   THE POOR LAW IN BOLTON PARISH

2.1   Early Provisions

In 1535 the Parish of Bolton le Moors was made responsible for the *'poor and impotent'* and the giving of private alms was forbidden. At least two able persons were appointed in 1563 to collect charitable donations and in 1572, when a compulsory poor rate was introduced, the office of overseer of the poor was created. By 1597 a Poor Rate for Indoor and Outdoor Relief was allowed which financed a Poor House for the incapacitated poor and work was found for able-bodied paupers. An extract taken from a Quarter Sessions Order Book of 1648 shows an order sent by the justices to *'the Churchwardens and Overseers of the Poor within the Parish of Bolton'* asking them *'to take special care and provide for the impotent, lame, poor and little orphans of poor people'* etc. Probably about this time, during the Civil War, administration in Bolton had become strained and the authorities needed to be reminded of their duties. The justices repeatedly pointed out that all hamlets or townships must share equally the burden of the poor in the whole parish. Despite considerable resistance to raising the necessary revenue, the justices provided the required *'Houses of Correction'* in Lancashire, first at Preston, then at Manchester in 1657. Both establishments were well used after the amendments to the 1662 Act.

In 1659, the Churchwarden of Bolton charged his Poor Account with the costs of attending the Quarter Sessions for a warrant to remove one Robert Nochols and his children back to Eccles, their legal settlement. In 1707 several of the inhabitants of the Manor of Little Bolton were presented at the Lord's Court for the offence of *'receiving and entertaining'* into their houses persons not having a legal settlement in the manor and not possessing a certificate of settlement. The following year the same Court ordered that tenants guilty of the offence should *'forfeit and pay the Lord of this Manor the sume of 15 shillings'*.

In 1760 one William Norris, a rogue and vagabond, who had broken his indentures and subsisted himself by begging and strolling up and down the country was passed through Bolton after his ejection from Liverpool on his way to his legal place of settlement in Great Lever, where the overseers were required to receive and provide for him. Evidence of this case can be found in a hand-written Vagrancy Notice in Bolton Parish Church records, giving details of the examination, taken on oath on 13 December, 1760. The Notice says:

'that he (Norris) *was found an apprentice to John Oldham of Great Lever, near Bolton le Moors in the County of Lancaster, craftsman by indenture for 7 years but only served 6 years and a half there, and had been acknowledged to belong to the township of Great Lever by the officers thereof, and have been relieved. His place of settlement is Great Lever as aforesaid. Although he was ordered to return to his settlement and was driven*

out of Liverpool, he did not return to Gt. Lever but subsisted himself since by begging and strolling up and down the country'. The document was sworn before John Blackburn, junior and William Norris appended his mark.

2.2   Effects of the 1834 Act

Those who drafted the 1834 Act did not entirely understand the sort of economy or society that the Industrial Revolution had produced in Lancashire and the requirement to enter a workhouse for relief could not always be adhered to. Bolton Poor Law Union was formed on 1 February 1837. In face of local opposition, the Assistant Poor Law Commissioner assured the Bolton Union Guardians in 1838 that they could continue to grant outdoor relief. The Union continued to give aid in money in periods of depression, as it was understood that when times improved, the people would be ready to take up work again in the mills. Had they been sent to the workhouse and their homes vacated, an immediate return to work would have been almost impossible. The workhouse test was therefore only applied to such people as incorrigible paupers, single women with illegitimate children and wandering Irish.

Early radicals believed the workhouse test to be a monstrous feature of the new Poor Law. Families would be split up on entry and sent to different buildings, where they would be confined until released. The editor of the Bolton Chronicle wrote: *'the new workhouses are like so many new prisons'*. Mr Edward Stanley, Whig candidate for South Lancashire considered outdoor relief to be necessary in Lancashire: *'for such sudden revolutions in trade occurred that in 24 hours a labour force might become destitute and a workhouse at large needed and numerous, or their cotton mills would be necessary to house them all'*. It was in the face of such opposition that the Assistant Poor Law Commissioner allowed outdoor relief. During periods of distress, outdoor relief was also given on a large scale to children. In 1848 it was estimated that 60,000 children were relieved in the Lancashire Unions. Some 15 years later, during the cotton famine, there were Unions each giving outdoor relief to at least 5000 children. Although the weekly relief, usually in the order of 6d-12d per head kept a child alive, it did little more.

In 1848, when nearly 30% of the population of Greater Bolton, Little Bolton and Tonge-with-Haulgh were on outdoor relief, the three townships joined together and undertook to construct a reservoir for Bolton Waterworks Company by employing their own paupers. In 8 months they lost £1901-7s-8d, having paid out more in wages than was received for the work. A month later the scheme was abandoned as there

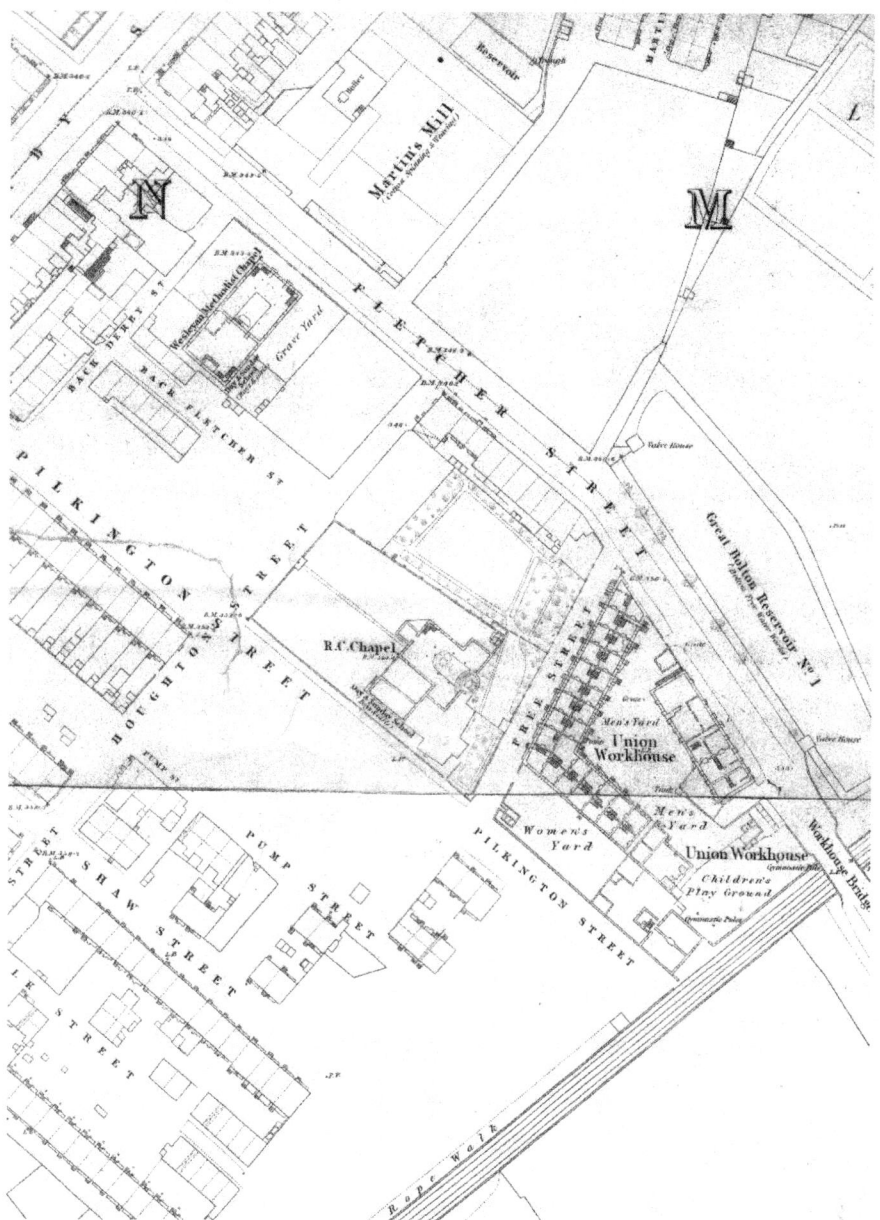

Map of 1847 showing the old Fletcher Street Workhouse in Bolton. The building was taken over by the Bolton Union under the 1834 Law and remained their main establishment until Fishpool was built.

were constant labour troubles. A similar situation occurred in 1857 when paupers were employed in preparing the site for building the new Fishpool Workhouse at Farnworth. Trouble flared up because the paupers were only given outdoor relief, rather than proper wages, and they resolutely refused to work.

The Bolton Union inherited their largest building, Fletcher Street Workhouse, from the township. The cottages were mainly grouped around a men's yard and the women had a separate yard. At Christmastime in 1842 it was full. 300 paupers occupied its buildings, crammed 20 to 25 to each cottage. There were only 119 beds in all, so families slept together in one bed as they would have done at home, the single beds being reserved for fever patients. Single men and women were kept in separate accommodation. Run on the family system each cottage had a day room downstairs, and there were rooms for washing and cooking. Children under the age of 10 years were sent to infant school morning and evening; and the older ones attended Sunday School. Most adults were employed in picking old rope for oakum. Some women did the cleaning or acted as nurses and men acted as barbers or did jobs outside such as mangle turning and road mending. From August 1842 no resident pauper was allowed back into the house after 7pm and no leave was granted or church attendance allowed because many made for the ale houses and came back drunk.

An example of the punishment of a pauper in Bolton Workhouse, approved and confirmed by the Board, was recorded on 6 Feb 1856. The master reported in the Pauper Offence Book that William Scholes, an inmate aged 54 years, had used insulting and obscene language in his presence and that of other inmates. He was given 8 oz of bread for his dinner instead of 4 oz of beef, 1 lb potatoes, 1 pint of broth & 3 oz of bread

Although there was a degree of liberty in the workhouses, overcrowding often brought chaos and unsanitary conditions. A Hansard report of an investigation in 1843 by an Assistant Poor Law Commissioner into the death of a pauper in Fletcher Street Workhouse outlines the appalling conditions. The workhouse, built in 1810/11 consisted of 13 cottages, the inmates of which were recorded. For example, in one cottage with 4 beds were a man and wife aged 38 and 40, their 3 children (aged 14, 7, and 2), 3 unmarried women aged 20-30 and 7 orphan children. In another cottage with 4 beds were a woman of 80, a man and wife aged 39, their 3 children (all under 10), a woman aged 40 with 3 children under 8, another woman aged 40 and 2 orphans aged 12 and 16. The inmates were verminous and there was no attempt to separate the sick from the healthy.

The Guardians agreed with an enquiry that single men and women could get together. In one instance a single women had been in the workhouse for 40 years and had given birth to two children. Following an earlier attempt to separate unmarried men from unmarried women the Bolton Chronicle had complained of the beginning of the '*bastille system'* in the township. In 1853 the Poor Law Inspector noted in the Bolton Workhouse Visiting Book that *'there is no classification by day or night'*.

Before 1834 Turton Workhouse had split up husbands and wives on entry, but the strictness decreased after the takeover by the Bolton Guardians. Families continued to live together despite Regulation 99 of the 1847 Act, which stated that only couples over the age of 60 were to remain together. An attitude prevailed that workhouses were also poor houses and retreats for the poor, as shown in Rochdale's workhouses where for many years inmates could have their own furniture, crockery and other possessions with them. They were also able to stay in the workhouse while they worked at outside employment and often paid for their food and accommodation.

On 13 Feb 1856 a Notice of Motion was entered by one Mr Stott to the Bolton Board of Guardians for the consideration of a new workhouse. The Chairman moved: *'that advertisements for plans for a new workhouse be inserted in newspapers for the best plans for a new building that shall accommodate 1000 Inmates, the cost not to exceed £18 per head.'*

The Commissioners had urged the construction of a single workhouse for the whole of the Union and although resistance to such a *'bastille'* was slow to die, the new project was slowly advanced. Eventually a new Bolton Union Workhouse at Fishpool, Farnworth was completed in 1861 which lived up to the ideals of the New Poor Law. Its inmates were classified and uniformed, disciplined and well-worked, although the nature of the work had not changed. The general workhouse test when applied was in the shape of rope oakum picking, wood chopping and corn grinding. Inmates were cleaner, healthier and adequately fed, so there was less determination to leave the place. The workhouse was well staffed with a chaplain, a school master and school mistress in addition to a master and mistress for general management. Useful skills were taught including tailoring, weaving and mat-making, and the workhouse had its own chapel and cemetery.

The Unions in Lancashire industrial areas, by patient firmness, closure orders and the influence of the inspectors built, or were building, new central workhouses by 1871; but only after most of the Guardians tried every tactic to save the old township workhouses. By 1871 the worst fears of the 1834 Act had not been realized. In most Lancashire towns outdoor relief continued as before, there was no general workhouse test or outdoor labour test for the genuine unemployed applicant and relief was still given in cash.

2.3 Connections Between Local Workhouses

In October 1820 a resolution was passed at Halliwell Workhouse that the undermentioned men be appointed to visit Turton Workhouse: James Crompton, John Makinson, William Makant, and James Sharples to observe Turton's methods of treating paupers. Halliwell paupers had previously been sent to workhouses at Brindle and Burnden but from this period some were probably sent to Turton. The Turton Registers include some Halliwell names and have references to paupers coming from there.

In addition to the relationship with Bolton Workhouse, links were also maintained between Turton and other workhouses in nearby townships, particularly with those in Harwood, Entwistle and Brindle.

During the period 1768 to 1784 regular weekly rent payments of 6s-6d were made by the township of Longworth to Brindle Workhouse, situated about one mile from the centre of Brindle village. Brindle took in the poor of any township that chose to contribute towards the support of their workhouse. There were about 80 townships in England that sent their poor to Brindle. A year's cost for an inmate was £11-18s-0d or about 4s-7d per week.

For many years Brindle was used as a general receptacle for pauper lunatics; also the idle and refractory poor of other townships were sent there. A severity of discipline was thus introduced at Brindle which was only alleviated when the county asylum, Lancaster Lunatic Asylum, was opened on Lancaster Moor in 1816. Its annex completed in 1882 cover an area of 41 acres and had a fine dining hall. Detainees were housed there until the early 20th century. It was renamed Lancaster Moor Hospital under the NHS.

> *'The inmates of Brindle Workhouse, to the number of one hundred and eleven, were on Christmas Day made the objects of the kind benevolence of the Guardians of the Poor. The dinner, as in former years, consisted of good English fare - beef and pudding. The humble party highly enjoyed themselves and expressed the strongest sense of respect and thankfulness to the kind donors by whose bounty their hearts had been so gratefully gladdened.'*
>
> *Preston Pilot and County Advertiser 31 December 1853*

> **Brindle Workhouse** operated on this site from 1734 to 1871.
>
> Originally taken over from a catholic mass house, the workhouse buildings were expanded and rebuilt housing over 200 'paupers and lunatics' until 1816. It was notorious for its severity and poor conditions even among workhouses, and took paupers from over 80 township across Lancashire. Around 1842 it was absorbed into the Chorley Poor Law Union and effectively became the towns main workhouse until its closure in 1871 with the building of the new workhouse at Eaves Lane.
>
> Among the thousands of paupers who must have passed through its doors were –
>
> W. Warner of Biston   Alexander Fowler   John Heywood
> Kitty Parker   George Blackstone   Jervis Hewson
> James Warburton   Alice Bennison   Timothy Cross
>
> Each was a person with their own story.
> For most of them, this is their only memorial.

Small inscription in concrete in a wall at the site of Brindle Workhouse.

Public hostility to the 1834 Poor Law led to this riot and
attack on Stockport Workhouse in 1842.

The old Doffcocker Inn, formerly Halliwell Township Workhouse.

Lancaster Moor Asylum: the datestone over the entrance reads MDCCCXVI.

CHAPTER III THE POOR LAW IN TURTON: c1730 to 1829

3.1 The Townships

Turton was fortunate in that it benefited from the Chetham Charity which enabled a large and lasting workhouse to be established at Goose Cote Hill.

Otherwise provision for the poor had to be made on a township by township basis before 1834. Hence Longworth, Entwistle, Harwood, Bradshaw, Edgworth, and Quarlton were each responsible for their own poor. Some townships acquired their own workhouses and some of the buildings still exist.

Harwood's workhouse was situated in Davenport Fold, an area whose population had increased in size during the late 1700s. Four of six cottages were interconnected with doorways and used as a workhouse until 1837 when inmates were temporarily removed to Turton Workhouse then on to Fishpool in Farnworth in 1861. By 1841 five of the cottages were occupied by hand-loom weavers, the other probably being used as part of the Harwood Township Offices.

Entwistle's workhouse was situated on Blackburn Road at Round Barn midway between Wayoh Bridge and Grimehills Bridge. In the mid-18th century the township overseer was Hugh Entwistle (the younger) and Ralph Entwistle was the constable. By 1750 there was great poverty and destitution in the township. The more prosperous families contributed to a rate for relieving the poor, some of whom might be housed in the workhouse. New skills were taught which helped inmates to make the transition from traditional hand-loom weaving to machine operation as the industrial revolution progressed.

At a meeting of the inhabitants of Longworth township on May 1 1784 an agreement was made that one John Whittle *'took upon himself to execute the office of Overseer of the Poor for the said township of Longworth for a period of 11 years, or for so long of that time as he shall live in the said township, for the yearly sum of two pounds ten shillings, for which said sum, one pound one shilling is to be paid by those whose turn it is to serve in the said office and the remainder which is one pound nine shillings is to be taken out of the tax yearly. But if anything be found which is not right in the accounts, then the said township may if they think fit, find another substantial householder to serve in the said office,'* this agreement was signed by several inhabitants. It was a case of appointing a substitute overseer of the poor to be paid partly by those who should have executed the office themselves and partly by the poor rate.

The property on the left is the former Entwistle Workhouse, attached to it is the former Duke of Wellington Inn, at Round Barn, Entwistle.

Davenport Fold, Harwood: the cottages on the right comprised the Harwood Workhouse and Township Offices during the early 1800s.

3.2 The Chetham Charity

Around 1736 Samuel Chetham, great nephew of Humphrey, gave an estate called Goose Cote Hill in the township of Turton to trustees for a term of 3 lives or 31 years. The rents were to be used for the benefit of the poor of Turton. The land included a farmhouse which had the potential to become the nucleus of a workhouse. A 1746 Survey valued the estate £4-10s-0d pa for the farmhouse, two pastured fields, a corn field, two other fields and 3 little meadows.

By Indentures of Lease and Release dated 1st and 2nd June 1748 Humphrey Chetham (brother of Samuel) left the Goose Cote Hill land and buildings in perpetuity to the township of Turton. The estate was conveyed to trustees John Wilson and John Lomax and their heirs in consideration of the trust that Chetham had in them. The estate consisted of a messuage and tenement (farmhouse with outbuildings and land), with a cottage, garden, and enclosed fields etc. The enclosed fields were known by the names, Nearer and Further Barn Field, Rough Field, Furthermost Field, Great Field, Meadow under the House, Middlemost and Furthermost Meadows, and Fold, comprising about 8 Cheshire Acres of land. The inhabitants of Turton built an extension on the farmhouse to act as a workhouse to house around 60 people. The cost was £64-7s-9d besides gift work. John Wood and John Orrell paid £20-0s-0d from the local rates and Samuel Holt, Overseer of the Poor, laid out £39-3s-0½d from the townships's money. The rents and profits were to be used for the support of poor people living or legally settled in Turton, whether already relieved by public assessment or not; relief to be given as the trustees should think fit.

One month later, by an indenture deed of 1 July 1748, John Wilson and John Lomax conveyed the estate to John Nuttall, John Orrell and John Wood who became the new trustees. The conveyance included an agreement to dispose of the rents and profits for the relief of the poor people of the township, in accordance with the wishes of the testator. Some of the rents and profits were spent by the trustees in the purchase of clothing for the poor and the families of many deserving and industrious people who were struggling to sustain themselves above the level of pauperism. The 1748 Indenture required that the trustees should meet twice a year in the Chapel of Turton or elsewhere, on Whit Monday and the first Monday after Christmas, for transacting necessary business as well as to elect poor people to receive the Charity. All transactions were entered in a book kept for the purpose. It was also agreed that whenever the number of trustees should fall to two, the two survivors would nominate others to make up their total number into four. Newly elected trustees had to reside and be legally settled in the manor, and the sitting survivors conveyed the premises to both the use of themselves and the new trustees.

A further development occurred in 1781 when a Memorandum of Agreement was made between John Wood and John Orrell, trustees and Samuel Holt, Overseer of the Poor, together with some of the principal inhabitants assembled at a Town Meeting held at Chapeltown on 7 Aug 1781. The Memorandum was worded: *Whereas a house was built last year (1780) at the north-east end of Goose Cote Hill Barn at the expense of Samuel Holt, Overseer of the Poor, on behalf of the landowners of the township of Turton, and John Wood and John Orrell, trustees for that estate, called Goose Cote Hill, first given by Samuel Chetham for 3 lives or 31 years, and then after given by Humphrey Chetham, land forever to be disposed of by the trustees, according to the conditions mentioned in the original deeds, to the poor of the township of Turton.*

The house at the end of the barn was seemingly to be a series of cottages with loomshops for use by the poor. The intention of the 1781 meeting was that John Wood, John Orrell and others should have the new building at the north-east end of the barn as a house within the estate forever, the proceeds to be used to provide cloth for the poor. The township churchwardens, overseers of the poor, and others had the benefit of the older buildings built in 1748 together with the original adjoining farmhouse and adjacent road, fold, coal house, little house and garden. This with extensions, was to be expanded into a *'house of industry'* (workhouse) administered by church wardens and overseers; Wood and Orrell giving up all control. A further change occurred in 1786 when by an Indenture of July 19 1786, trustees John Orrell and John Wood conveyed their premises (the barn and new house) to Isaac Orrell (son of John Orrell) and John Ashworth (son of Henry Ashworth) as their successors, who became the trustees in office.

The original farmhouse and extensions were in the tenancy of a Richard Isherwood during 1792/93. A letter dated 7 December 1793 signed by John Howarth as agent for the landlords, gave notice to Isherwood to remove and quit as he was overholding the buildings and land, and would have to pay double the yearly value after the date of the notice.

This was a time when great panic occurred and the rates in Turton were 10 shillings in the pound. Economic conditions were poor; bad harvests and turmoil in Europe caused a loss of overseas markets which resulted in high food prices and little work. Unemployment was high and many were thrust into the house which was inhabited by some of the worst of characters.

An *'Account Book'* of 1794 shows how the income was collected. It was kept by the trustees, Isaac Orrell and John Ashworth for an *'aforesaid pious use'*. The money collected became known as the Humphrey Chetham Charity (HCC) and provided cloth and bed linen to help the poor and elderly people who were not actually paupers dependent on the township.

Order from Isaac Orrell for cloth for a pauper child.

3.3 The Nineteenth Century

Mobility between townships was active during the early nineteenth century. Examples of Legal Settlements in Turton approved by the justices include: a certification of December 1829 that *'the child or children of one Alice Crook, wife of absentee Albert Crook and settled in Turton, will when born be legally settled in Turton Township'*, and another of November1831 that *'the child or children of one Mary Brooks, a pregnant spinster settled in Turton, would when born be legally settled in Turton Township'*.

The original farmhouse and extensions became by successive enlargements the Turton Workhouse. The legal proceedings were as follows: In 1801, it was found necessary to incur considerable expense in adapting the old house to its new purpose, which was met by public subscription. At a Township Meeting on 31 January 1801 at the house of trustee John Nuttall, three collectors of subscriptions were appointed for the Lower End of the Township (Edward Best, John Ashworth and James Haslam) and three for the Higher End (John Kershaw, Simon Lomax & James Kay), James Brandwood was to be Treasurer. Vestry (decision-making) meetings were frequently held and at one on 22 June 1801, improvements at Goose Cote Hill were considered when it was agreed to contribute money according to the extent of ownership or occupation of land. The sum of £238-4s-6d was raised, voluntary subscriptions included: *'John Carter from his premises in Turton, £10; and Joseph Brandwood from his Corn Mill, £10'*.

Below is a signed estimate dated 14 January 1801 written at the Globe Inn, Turton, giving the probable expense of the alterations and improvements at Goose Cote Hill.

	£	s	d
Getting and carting Stones for the Buildings and Garden walls	10	0	0
36 Windles for Lime for Masons and Plasterers	4	1	0
6 Cartloads of Sand at 3/6 per yd	1	1	0
Timber for Lintels in several places and two gates	1	1	0
50 Yards of deal board for doors etc.	2	1	0
Deal Uprights for Partitions above Stairs	3	3	0
4 pair of new Door Cheeks bound	1	6	0
Chimney piece and Window Stones	1	8	0
46 Yards of Parpoint wall at 1/- per yd.	2	6	0
Cutting the cross passage thro the inner Gable ends and securing all the chimney draughts above	7	7	0
Walling up thro Front doors and altering windows in the Loomshop	4	3	0
Hewing a Chimney piece and walling a new Draught in the Kitchen	2	2	0
Tearing nails, common nails, hinges, handles, etc	1	8	0
Carpenter's work in making partitions, Stairs, Doors, Lintels, etc	3	10	0
Two Thousand of Tearing Laths	3	12	0
Iron work for two gates	4	7	0
Plaister work, pointing etc.	4	14	0
Hair--40 Strikes	2	0	0
Draining the Garden Land	2	10	0
Walling the Garden and Front Walls, 26 perches at 3/6 each	4	11	0
Supposed expense of the Back Kitchen, Coalhouse and Necessary	43	0	0
Sub total	109	11	0
The Furnishing of the whole Workhouse in a proper manner may not cost less than	100	0	0
Total	209	11	0

On 14 February 1801, John Howard was contracted to do the masonry work for the back kitchen, a coal house and *'two necessaries'* (privies). The kitchen was to be 3.5 yards high from the *'Cod Stones to the Square'*, and the other buildings were to be 2.5 yards high from the threshold to the Square; *'to do the same in a handsome and substantial manner equal to Jas Crook the Miller's House'*. The kitchen work had to be completed by 15 April, and the other buildings by the 12 May (or forfeit 2d per yard for all the walls.) Thomas Slater, John Sudren, Samuel Knowles, and James Crook were to superintend the work in their turns on a weekly basis.

In May 1816 the new farm buildings and land, held by the trustees, were to be let by ticket at £34-10s pa and a note to that effect was entered in the account book. There were 7 bidders. The property was let to James Horrocks, the sitting tenant and highest bidder, for 14 years.

The rent received by the trustees was spent on linen and cloth, and distributed among those poor of Turton who did not receive a constant parochial relief. The number of recipients varied between 70 and 90 each year, and the length of cloth given to each person varied from 3 to 12 yds. Distribution was on Whit Friday and Christmas Day. John Ashworth, a trustee, bought Drogheda linen wholesale from John Cross of Bolton in 1821 for this purpose.

By Indentures of Aug 12 1823 John Ashworth conveyed the estate to Thomas Wood, Henry Ashworth and John Ashworth the younger, with the same powers and conditions as were contained in the original deeds of 1748.

At a meeting of ratepayers and landowners on 30 December 1824, chaired by John Ashworth, it was agreed that *'greater convenience'* was wanted in *'The House'*, and this would be to great advantage to the township. Hence it was agreed to borrow £400 and charge it to the Poor Rate. The signatories John Ashworth, John Kershaw, James Crook, Thomas Wood, John Knowles, John Ashworth Jnr. and Peter Haslam were appointed to borrow the said sum and prepare a plan of the premises for the money to be spent on alterations.

At a meeting held on 5 Feb 1825 it was agreed to give Oliver Ormrod the sum of 10d per superficial yard for *'building the pig coat and necessaries'* (privies) from the plan produced and 8d per superficial yard for the fence wall in front of the present house. The fence wall was to be 2 ft 6in broad at the bottom and 1 ft 4 in broad at the top. It was also agreed to provide dressed stones and other wall stones for a new coal house *'it to be equal in workmanship to the present coalhouse'*. John Kershaw was engaged to cart the necessary lime from Blackburn for 4d per load.

At a further meeting held on 1 March 1825 Oliver Ormrod was authorised to sink the foundations for the coal house at 6d per cubic yard, the soil to be taken into the garden in front of the *'new necessaries'*. Also included was the carting of all the sand needed for the new buildings except for the flagging. All the outside walls were to be dressed with road sand of the best quality. On March 2 1825 Oliver Ormrod was authorised to convert the dungeon or cell, the walls were to be parpoint, not less than 12 inches thick, well coursed, squared in the joints, and built at the price of two shillings per superficial yard.

Goose Cote Hill FARM,
TO BE LET,

For a Term of Years,

AT THE WORK-HOUSE, IN TURTON,

ON THURSDAY, 5th NOVEMBER, 1829,

AT THREE O'CLOCK IN THE AFTERNOON,

ALL THAT FARM,

SITUATE AT GOOSE COTE HILL,

CONTAINING EIGHT CHESHIRE ACRES OF

Meadow and Pasture LAND,

WITH A GOOD

FARM-HOUSE,

AND OUT BUILDINGS.

For particulars apply to JOHN ASHWORTH, Jun. or THOMAS WOOD, of Turton.

TURTON, OCTOBER 12TH, 1829. [J. OGLE, PRINTER, BOLTON.

Notice for letting Goose Cote Hill Farm.

Receipt for cloth bought for the poor.

THE LORD'S DAY PLAN of the Methodist Preachers in the Bolton Circuit. 1818.

In meekness instructing those that oppose themselves 2 Tim. 2. 25.

Places	June			July				August				Sept		No.	PREACHERS
	Time 10½.6	21 1	28 2	5 1	12 2	19 1	26 2	2 6	9 2	16 1	23 2	30 1	6 2	13 1	1	G. Highfield
Bolton New Chapel	2½	2	1	2	1	2		2 5	2	1	2	1		2	2	Jon. Turner
Do. Do.		2	1	3	1	2 4		2	2	1	2		1	2	3	J. Twist
															4	J. Taylor
Do Old Chapel	8	6	2	12	5	19	9	18 3	13	11	10		6	12	5	T. Taylor
Halshaw Moor		6	4	6	2	18	3 3	14 16	2	15	11	1		10	6	J. Musgrave
															7	R. Dawson
Little Lever	3	6	12	18 1	4	6	13	9	17 2	11	18	5	3	10 14	8	J. Crompton
															9	J. Bolton
Horwich		6	11	10	16	1	1	11	5	18	4	17 2	13	9	10	D. Lyon
Edgworth		5	6	11	14	13	2	16	18	10	5	1	9	13	11	R. Bolton
Turton Workhouse		3.7	16		8		4		11		7		13	17	12	T. Broadbelt
and Birtinshaw															13	J. Atkins
Brightmet		7	9	5	12	10	17	6	4	13	14	16 18	3	2	14	J. Chapman
Chew Moor		2		4		9		13	11		10		12		15	J. Summers
Hawkshaw Lane		4½	13		7		10		8		16	15		18	16	J. Wood
Harwood Lee		7	10		3		12		16		9	4		5	17	G. Ellidge
Ainey Bridge		6	8		11		5		12		6	14		4	18	T. Aspinall
Dixon Green		6	7		13		18		9		11	8		10		
Colliers Row		6		9		8		14		7		18		17		Supernumeraries.
Finets		6	13		17		9		10	8		6		7		J. Beswick
Durnden		7	13		4		11		7	12		11		3		T. Brandwood
Lever Mills		6		3	3		8		15		12	7				
Belmont		2		13	17		7		14		8	16				
Markland Hill		6	7		3		15		8		6	5		8		
Chequebent		6½	13		15		16		13	18		7				
Roper's Bath		6½		1		12	17		9	4		15				
Cottage Hillison		6½				4	18		6	3		9		6		
Wingates		10½	2	5			14			3						

THE LORD'S SUPPER
At Bolton on the last Lord's-day in every month
Halshaw Moor July 5th

Baptisms
First Lord's-day in every month immediately after the Forenoon Service, Parents or requested to give notice to the Chapel-keeper in the Morning and they must be present.

Quarterly Sermon
To the Children of the Sunday School, June 28
Quarterly Meeting Thursday June 25th

Lovefeast at BOLTON July 5th
The Local Preachers meeting at 8 o'clock
Old Chapel Vestry August 31st.

N.B. If a preacher cannot attend his place he must get it supplied by one whose name is on the Plan, unless he be confined by sickness or be on a Journey.

No. 8 9 10 11 to attend the next Watch-Night July 6th

A Missionary Prayer Meeting the first Thursday in every Month.

N.B. The July Collection to be made in every the 2nd Sunday in July or on the 5th.

The Bolton Circuit Lords Day Methodist Preachers' Plan of 1818, showing that preachers shared between Birtenshaw Chapel and Turton Workhouse.

A Vestry Meeting was held on 25 June 1825 to assess the needs of the township's poor. Present were: John Ashworth (chairman), George Slater, John Kershaw, James Crook, John Ashworth Jnr, Peter Ormrod, John Knowles, Thomas Wood, Samuel Holt, George Howarth and Oliver Ormrod. It was resolved unanimously that the proceedings from previous meetings about the workhouse enlargement be approved and to borrow £500 instead of £400. The inhabitants and occupiers were to be assessed as before. It was further resolved, by two-thirds of all the assessed inhabitant and occupiers, that the churchwardens and overseers of the poor should raise the £500 by means of a loan from Mr John Heywood of Little Bolton, the wardens and overseers being authorised to sign the necessary securities. Two further sums of £31 from William Sharples, Workhouse Master, and £60 from John Knowles, were also borrowed, making a total of £591 against future poor rates. A letter written by William Sharples in 1827 exonerated one Robert Nuttall as not being turned out of the workhouse on account of being the writer or indicter of a letter.

In 1825-1827, a time of great stagnation of trade with a diminishing market for woven products, it became necessary to enlarge the workhouse. At that time the principal employment of Turton's poor was hand-loom weaving, a trade that gradually declined as power-loom weaving expanded. The poor weavers had no access to power looms and there was little else for them to do. The ratepayers, following discussions at length, decided to adopt a system of workhouse employment with extensive provision for hand-loom weaving. A *'labour test'* was devised to prevent the fostering of idleness and select those who might enter the house as the best way of tiding them over a period of difficulty.

The Ashworth family, industrialists in the Turton area from the late 18th century, continued to take an interest in the workhouse, partly to safeguard their own interests as large rate payers. John Ashworth of The Oaks, Bradshaw, was a Trustee from 1786 and in 1823 Henry and John Ashworth Jnr both joined him.

At one time, during a period of trade stagnation, it was proposed to give a spade and wheelbarrow to paupers and get them to dig sand from a hill being lowered for a turnpike road. However, from a group of 32 inmates only 4 were found suitable for such work and 3 of these gave up within 2 days. At that time the workhouse became known, perhaps unfairly, as '*Ashworth's Mill*' where paupers were sent *'to be ground'*. Although the Ashworth family were hard task-masters and strict, they supported fair treatment for the paupers.

Paupers from neighbouring areas were admitted to Turton Workhouse and the Turton *'labour test'* was offered to them at an economic charge. The promoters of the scheme were ably supported by the energetic Master, William Sharples and the threat of the increasing expense of pauperism was greatly reduced.

The industrial skills of most of the inmates were expected to be retained until more prosperous times, when they could again become householders and resume responsibility for their families. During the times when handloom weaving was available for fit inmates, it was intended they would leave the workhouse with improved habits and be fit to make their own way in the world. However it should have been clear that handloom weaving was a declining trade and those that followed it were increasingly unlikely to subsist.

Some paupers were brought from further afield, for example a group from Bledlow in Buckinghamshire were brought to Egerton in 1834. Bledlow was a centre for corn milling and it was thought inhabitants might have experience of machinery. They travelled by coach or wagon from their parish to London and then from Paddington to Manchester by canal on a Pickford's boat. Henry Ashworth took four families recommended for their honesty and sobriety, totalling 37 people with a number of single men and girls. There were 11 southern families in all. Local workers lent the immigrants furniture, pans and kettles.

An example of a 'cloth dole', in which lengths of cloth were distributed among the poor, 1819.

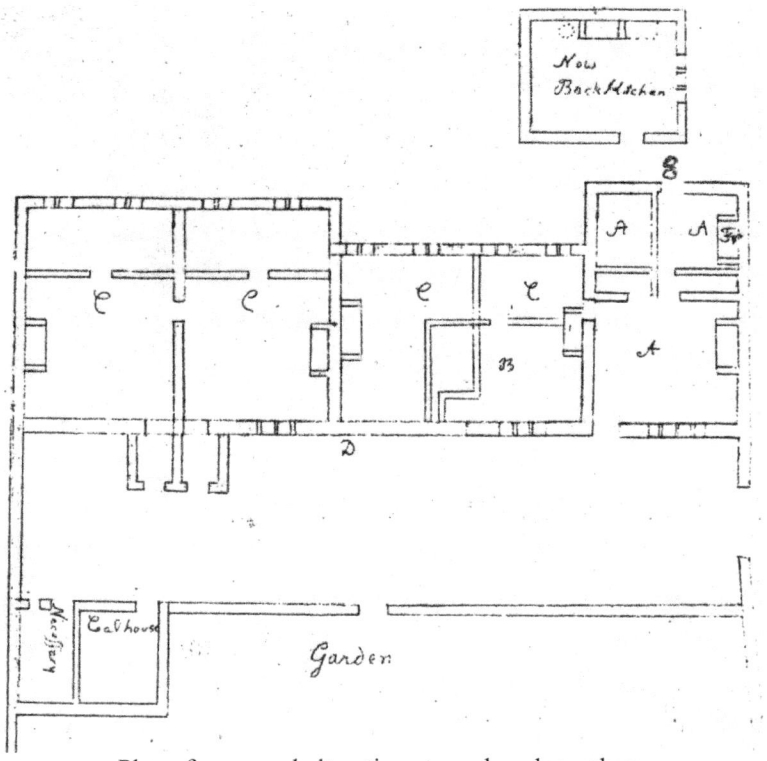

Letter from William Sharples, Workhouse Master at Goose Cote.

Plan of proposed alterations to make a loomshop.

In a period of unemployment the workhouse buildings were to be altered to make provision for hand-loom weaving. Some of the partitions were to be removed and others erected. The new loomshop (CCCC) was to be open. A dining room (B) 3.5 x 3 yds was planned; a new back door (E) opened from the governor's kitchen (A) and a new *'fire draught'* put up in said kitchen (Fp). Also planned was a new kitchen built behind the governor's house and a coal house and *'necessary'* in the corner of the garden.

CHAPTER IV ACTIVE YEARS AT TURTON: 1830-1861

4.1 The 1830s

A Report by the Poor Law Commissioners in 1834 found that Turton Workhouse was *'well managed'*. Able-bodied paupers were offered entry and bathed and dressed in parish clothes, but not allowed outside without the Master's consent. As more work became available, the workhouse lost inmates. The capacity left unoccupied was then used to accommodate paupers from other townships. Some Lostock paupers were not taken into the nearby Westhoughton Workhouse but instead into Turton. Even though much further to travel, the conditions at Turton were better than at Westhougton, and there was a saving of 10d per head per week. Although it was admitted there was a hole in need of repair in the roof of Turton Workhouse during this period, there were three blankets on most beds. Mr Mott, the Commissioner, said so far as Turton was concerned he could most willingly bear testimony to the good order, the excellent fare and the satisfactory arrangements of the workhouse. Turton, he thought, was one of the best workhouses in England. It was attracting people from Little Bolton, Bradshaw, Breightmet, Entwistle, Harwood, Darcy Lever, Little Lever, Longworth, Lostock, Westhoughton, Tonge-with-Haugh, Farnworth, Heaton, Little Hulton, Middle Hulton, Over Hulton, Halliwell, Kearsley, and Rumworth.

The Bolton Union, formed in 1837, consisted of 26 townships in and around Bolton. In that year, two small workhouses were closed at Little Hulton and at Westhoughton and their inmates transferred to Bolton's Fletcher Street Workhouse and Turton Workhouse. A Guardians' Minute Book records for 15 April 1837 that Turton Workhouse was freehold, had a capacity for 90 inmates, and the master's salary was £35-0s-0d. The total number of inmates who belonged there were 3 men, 6 women, 4 boys under 13 and 3 girls under 13, making a total 16. In early 1839 Turton recorded 73 inmates. The cost per head per week was 2s 3¾d, the same as in Bolton.

In 1837 decisions about the alternatives of outdoor relief or the workhouse were left to the Guardians. Mr John Ashworth enquired if part of a family needing relief could be taken into the workhouse, rather than be admitted as a body. Also, whether aged widows, not able to support themselves, should be given outdoor relief, rather than thrust them into the workhouse. He thought the former would be more humane. The Commissioners instructed that where outdoor relief was granted to able-bodied persons, it should be partly given in provisions so that the money could not be misapplied, which all too frequently was the case. Some employment was also recommended for the able-bodied.

Map of the Parishes of Bolton-le-Moors and Deane divided into townships, together with Great Lever, an isolated part of the Parish of Middleton. The Bolton Union under the 1834 Poor Law comprised the whole of this area except for the townships (grey) of Rivington and Anglezarke (included in the Chorley Union) and Blackrod (included in the Wigan Union).

On 25 June 1839, following the establishment of the Bolton Union, the Board of Poor-Law Guardians rented, from the township, the whole of the workhouse buildings in Turton with all appurtenances for £50 pa. The Board of Guardians received a letter from Mr Andrew Bury of Egerton stating he had declined the post of Medical Officer to the Turton District on account of the smallness of the salary which was £35pa. The post was re-advertised at £40pa and Mr Bury again applied.

The year 1839 also saw the departure of the Workhouse Governor and his wife. A number of ratepayers met at the workhouse for the purpose of presenting the Governor and Matron with a silver plate teapot, coffee pot, cream jug, sugar tongs, 12 teaspoons, sugar spoon, and a China tea service set. The teapot was inscribed *'Presented to Wm and Dorothy Sharples by the ratepayers of the Township of Turton as an acknowledgement of their faithful services as Governor and Matron of the Turton Workhouse during a period of 21 years'*.

4.2 The 1840s

The 1841 census shows that Turton Workhouse staff included *'Robert Lowe, governor weaver and Elizabeth Lowe, matron'*. Over the 10 years, from 1840 to 1850, monies received from the Bolton Union for the use of the Turton Workhouse, together with the purchase money for the fixtures, repaid all the borrowed money with interest and arrears of interest, amounting to £661, yielding an eventual income of £50 pa to Turton township.

In October 1841 the master complained that the walls and roof needed repair. He was ordered to draw the attention of the Overseers, as owners, to the state of the building and request the necessary work be done. During December 1843 a sum of money not exceeding £10 was allocated to improve the ventilation of the building. In May 1844 two store pigs, one ladder, and 350 ft of 1 inch deal for repairing the floor was ordered. Approval was given for papering the governor's sitting room on 28 June 1844. On 11 April 1845 the estimate from Mr Wm Kenyon for the proposed alteration of the workhouse windows etc, amounting to £6-3s-0d was accepted. More work was ordered on 25 August 1845. The men's day room was to be repaired, the ceiling raised, the floors taken up and boarded over again, a partition fitted in the kitchen, a new parlour door provided and fixed, the spout and window frames painted, and a pair of clothing squeezers provided. More repairs followed during the following year.

Between 1842 and 1858 beds and bedding were bought for the workhouse. Six bedsteads were ordered on the 14th January 1842, and another 4 ordered the following April together with 4 cribs. Sheets and blankets were bought during 1852 at 12s-0d per pair, and iron bedsteads bought from James Howarth in October 1852 at £7-15s-

Schedule C.—FORM 13.

ADMITTED.

No. in Relief List	NAME	When Born	Parish to which belonging	Calling	PARTICULARS TO FILL UP THE PAUPER DESCRIPTION BOOK.				Cause of seeking Relief	Observations on condition at the time of Admission. Names of Relations liable under 43d Elizabeth, and any other general Remarks.	Number in Pauper Description Book	Of what Religious Persuasion
					If Admit, whether Single, Married, Widow or Widower; if Child, whether Orphan, Deserted or Bastard.	If able-bodied	If perfectly or wholly Disabled, and Cause of Disability.	If receiving any Relief from Clubs, Charitable Institutions, Government Pensions, or otherwise.				
1	Margret Chadwick	1790	Over Hulton	Weaver	Single	no			Soft			
2	Catherine Wolmesley	1821	D°	—	D°	no			Soft			
1	J.ª Chadwick	1787	D°	—	D°	no			D°			
1	J.ª Wright	1827	Farnworth	—	Widow	yes			Old Age			
1	J.ª Ratcliffe	1812	D°	Mason	Single	yes			D°			
1	Pet.ʳ Ratcliffe	1833	D°	Weaver	Widow	yes			Passport			
2	Willm Ratcliffe	1796	D°	Mason	Married	yes						
3	Joseph Heliwell	1809	D°	Weaver	D°	yes						
4	James Howard	1806	D°	D°	D°	yes						
2	Joseph Kelvint	1824	D°	D°	D°	no						
3	Mary Lainn	1831	D°	—	Married	no						
1	Lawrence Hartsen	1809	J. Mingle	—	yes				Factory			
1	R. A. Lowsley	1800	D°	Factory	yes							
2	M. A. Lowsley	1832	D°	—	yes							
1	Jn.º Lowsley	1798	D°	—	yes							
1	Mary Robinson	1799	Horton	Factory	yes							
1	Oliver Henderson	1813	Farnworth	Miner	no				Mines			
2	Jn.º Oppenshaw	1828	D°	—	no							
1	W.ᵐ Taylor	1747	Redwell	Widow	yes				Soft			
2	Rob.ᵗ Entwistle	1777	D°	—	yes							
1	Jno Greenhalgh	1825	D°	Miner	yes							
2	Catherine McJarge	1855	D°	Mines	yes							
3	J.º M.ªArg.ᵗ	1856	D°	—	yes				Teeth			

0d. An inventory of furniture and other effects was taken by the Master in February 1856 and examined by the clerk's assistant, Mr Cooper. More bedsteads were bought in January, April and May 1856, with quilts and sheets manufactured at Bolton Workhouse bought in November 1858.

One task given to male inmates in this period was stone-breaking. In November 1841 a stone-breaking bench was ordered and set up to break up stones for sand. Twelve hammers and one riddle were provided.

The Governor was directed to provide 10 suits of clothes for the inmates in January 1842, and in April 1843 a tender was sought from a Mr Peter Skelton for supplying the following:

Grey calico (a plain woven textile)	@ 2½d	per yd
Grey calico	@ 3d	per yd
Grey drabbetts (a twill weave linen fabric)	@ 4d	per yd
Drabbett shirts, linen neck and wrists	1s 11½d	each
Drabbett shirts	1s 4d	each
Calico shirts, linen neck and wrists	1s 7d	each
Calico shirts	1s	each
Men's hose	1s 2d a pair, 14sh per doz	
Shambras	@ 5½d	per yd
White flannel (a cotton fabric)	@ 11½d	per yd
Red flannel	@ 1s	per yd
Boys' clothes No3 4s 9d, to rise and fall 6d per size, the smaller 6d less, the sizes larger 6d more		
Women's black knit hose	10d, 1s, 1s 1d	
Olive twill drabbett	@ 5½d	per yd
Blue print	@ 4d	per yd
Blue linen	@ 7½	per yd
Check	@ 7d	per yd

A quotation for footwear from a Richard Barlow in June 1844 lists:

New clogs	3s 6d	per pair
Young men's clogs	3s	per pair
Women's clogs	2s 8d	per pair
Boys' and girls' clogs	2s	per pair
Small ones	1s 8d	per pair
Clogging, all sizes	9d	per pair

It was ordered that the allowance of tobacco and snuff to the aged inmates of Bolton and Turton workhouses be alike in quality and quantity, to a limit of half an ounce per head per week.

The subject of the employment of inmates was a cause for concern in 1843 when workhouse earnings were raised for picking oakum. Oakum picking consisted of unravelling and cleaning lengths of rope which caused hand-blistering and bleeding. This process involved pulling the strands and opening the rope. The oakum was re-used for caulking the seams of boats.

The Bolton Chronicle reported in 1834 that no inmate of a workhouse was to be obliged to attend any religious service contrary to his religious principles or have his children educated against his wishes. Dissenting clergy were given the right to minister at a workhouse when requested and in 1844 the Workhouse Committee was requested to provide Bibles for the use of inmates.

Tension must have existed between Mr Kay of Turton Tower and the Workhouse Governor. The boy inmates were put to work on odd jobbing and gardening in Turton Tower grounds. During 1839 the Governor wanted the boys to take sandwiches to the Tower for their dinner. But Mr Kay would not let them eat on the premises, so they had to trail backwards and forwards between the Tower and workhouse at dinner time. By April 1843 Mr Kay had complained to the Board that the Governor had not allowed some boys to return to work after dinner. The Board's Workhouse Committee presented a report of their investigation of the circumstances with a resolution that the Governor should be admonished in the presence of the Board. The admonition was done by the Board chairman.

A letter from the Poor Law Board (PLB) of 15 June 1849 was read which expressed approval for a plan for alterations and additions at Turton Workhouse, and requested, when the plan had been altered, that it might be sent for their formal approval. Seven tenders for the alterations were duly received; that of Robert Warburton of Egerton was for £320, but that of Robert Haslam of Bolton for £325 was accepted. A letter from the PLB dated 27 June 1849 accompanied the returned plan and observed that no access was shown to the boy's day room and recommended that it should be provided in such a way that the boys when going to and from that room would not be brought into contact with any other class of inmates. It was further suggested that a window be placed to light the hospital staircase, and that a water closet if required be provided on the landing of that staircase.

The 1851 census gives a total of 78 residents in the workhouse, the Master still being Robert Lowe. Further work was required on 14 May 1851 when a tender for slating etc, was accepted on condition that hair mortar be used. A sum of £12-9s-7d was paid for painting to Thomas Horrobin on 11 August 1852.

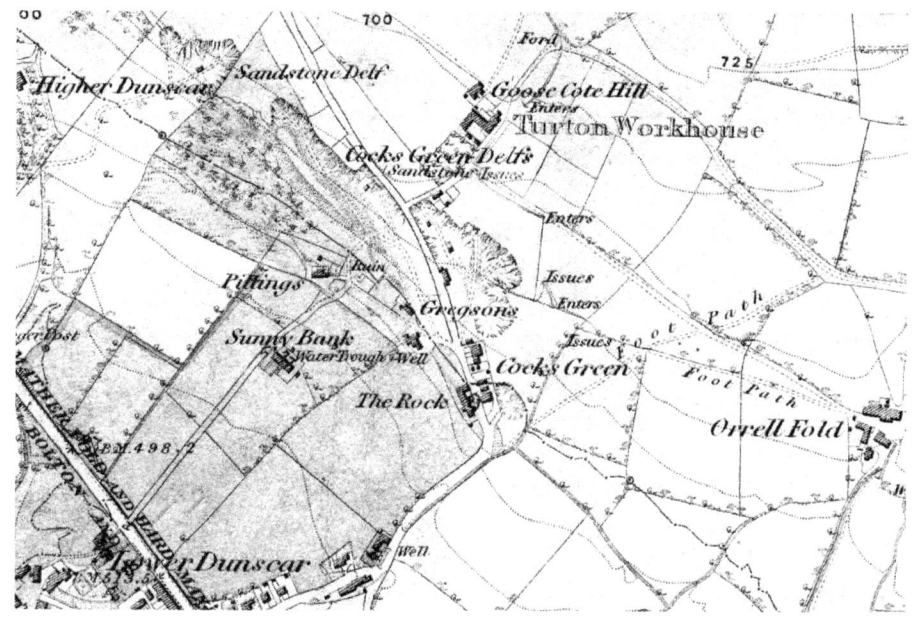

Six inch OS Map of 1848 showing Turton Workhouse.

NOTICE IS HEREBY GIVEN,

THAT

WE, the Overseers of the Poor of the Township of TURTON, have postponed the Meeting called for the 6th instant, and hereby request the Inhabitant Ratepayers to meet in

PUBLIC VESTRY

At the WORKHOUSE, on THURSDAY next,

The 12th July Instant,

AT 6 O'CLOCK IN THE EVENING.

When the business of the Overseers connected with the Township, will be then laid before such Meeting.

Dated this 6th day of JULY, 1849.

JOHN ASHWORTH, JUN. } OVERSEERS
WILLIAM HORROCKS } OF TURTON.

JOHN BURRELL, PRINTER, CROWN STREET, BOLTON.

Notice to 'Inhabitant Ratepayers' of a Public Vestry meeting on 12 July 1849 called by the Overseers at Turton Workhouse.

Cox Green Road in 1939 (upper) and 1910 (lower). Before c1800 this was the main road to Blackburn and for many years the route to Turton Workhouse.

4.3 The 1850s

The financial outlay on Turton Workhouse before 1825 was £361-15s-3½d. During the years 1826 and 1827 outlay for improvements and expansion was £594-8s-8d, and from March 1840 to March 1850 costs of repairs amounted to £45-17s-0d making expenditure from the commencement £1002-0s-11½d.

A letter from the PLB on the 22 September 1852 referred to increasing the number of inmates. Enclosed was a form requiring a detailed statement from the medical officer on the accommodation in each day room and sleeping room. Builders' tenders were read the following week for converting the building into a school for pauper children as follows: Wm Greenhalgh £55-0s-0d, John Murphy £56-10s-0d, and George Gaukroger £55-0s-0d. It was ordered that Mr Greenhalgh's tender be accepted and that the work proceed without delay. On 27 Oct 1852 an architect was employed to arrange for additional alterations at Turton, recommended by the Workhouse Committee; that a room be made over the 'dead house' for the purpose of keeping straw and that the present straw room at the end of the intended schoolroom be made into a drying room.

The PLB fixed the number of children at 150 in November, 1852 and the following month accepted the plan and estimates for the drying room. The Medical Officer having strongly advised on the preparation of the drying stove, Messrs. Musgraves, contractors, were authorised to erect it.

4.4 Food, Meals & Diet

Up to the mid 19th century, workhouse food was minimal and meals frequently had to be eaten in silence with the paupers seated in serried rows. The quantity of food was often less than that provided for a prisoner in jail, but improvements were made towards the end of the century as the New Poor Law began to operate.

During November 1841 it was ordered that the payment made to a woman to bake bread at Turton Workhouse should cease. If the woman's services were to be retained, the money should be charged to Turton Township to which she belonged. A baking oven capable of holding about 8 loaves was to be acquired and in May 1843 it was ordered that two workhouse pigs be cured for the paupers use. Two more pigs were ordered in June 1843. A few months later the workhouse committee recommended that, as most of the inmates were aged persons or small children, the diet should be changed a little and wheaten bread substituted for oat bread in certain cases, as considered advisable. The order for an oven, suggested in November 1841, was to be put into effect.

In August 1844 the Workhouse Committee suggested to the Board that the bread might be baked at Bolton Workhouse with profit to the Union. The suggestion was adopted. A substantial dinner with a reasonable allowance of beer, or coffee if preferred, was given to inmates at the following New Year's meal. From August 1848 breakfast at both Bolton and Turton workhouses was at 8am. During May 1852 it was recommended that the Governor of Turton Workhouse be allowed to substitute suet dumplings for rice twice a week.

An order for provisions for the workhouse, minuted in August 1852, is as follows:-

Richard Cunliffe	Bread	£1-3-0
Alfred Scowcroft	Beef	£16-5-0
Wright & Co	Snuff	£2-3-0
Thomas Almond	Potatoes	£5-6-0
James Lever	Sugar & Tobacco	£2-2-11
Henry Bromiley	Milk & Butter	£1-4-5
Samuel Orrell	Coals	£3-15-8

Black tea, green tea and coffee were bought later and Peter Higson supplied knives and forks for £1-16s-0d.

In March 1853 Mr Pendlebury, the Medical Officer, observed that pea soup was too purging for the children in Turton Workhouse and was asked by the Guardians to recommend a diet for children under 9 years. The recommendation was: for breakfast, bread and milk porridge as usual; for dinner, suet puddings 3 times a week, cooked meat with bread and vegetables twice a week and coffee with bread and butter twice a week; for supper, milk porridge for those above 4 years of age as usual and for those under 4 years of age a sufficient quantity of new milk. The Guardians accepted this except for the new milk, so blue milk was substituted. PLB approval was given. In March 1855, milk was obtained from the cows on the farm, and in May the provision included beer.

In August 1855 the Committee was requested to investigate a statement, alleged to have been made by the schoolmaster, that the inmate children at Turton were in the habit of picking up and eating potato peelings and turnip peelings on the highway and the committee should visit the workhouse to investigate.

During October 1855 the PLB requested written copies of workhouse diets which the clerk forwarded. When read, the PLB gave their sanction and approval on the understanding that the ingredients of the several articles of food should be as nearly as possible of the kinds and in the proportions set forth in the statements annexed to the dietary tables. It was ordered that copies of the above be printed and affixed on the wards of the workhouses.

DIETARY for Able-Bodied Men and Women

		Breakfast			Dinner			Supper		
		B	Gruel	Cooked meat	P	Soup	S	B	C	Broth
		oz	pints	oz	lb	pints	oz	o	oz	pints
Sun	M	6	1½	5	½	-	-	6	-	1½
	W	5	1½	5	½	-	-	5	-	1½
Mon	M	6	1½	-	-	1½	-	6	2	-
	W	5	1½	-	-	1½	-	5	2	-
Tue	M	6	1½	5	½	-	-	6	-	1½
	W	5	1½	5	½	-	-	5	-	1½
Wed	M	6	1½	-	-	1½	-	6	2	-
	W	5	1½	-	-	1½	-	5	2	-
Thur	M	6	1½	5	½	-	-	6	-	1½
	W	5	1½	5	½	-	-	5	-	1½
Fri	M	6	1½	-	-	-	14	6	2	-
	W	5	1½	-	-	-	12	5	2	-
Sat	M	6	1½	-	-	1½	-	6	2	-
	W	5	1½	-	-	1½	-	6	2	-

In the above table M = men, W = women, P = potatoes, B = Bread, C = Cheese
S = Suet or Rice Pudding

In Addition:

OLD PEOPLE of 60 years and upwards may be allowed 1oz of tea, 7oz of butter and 8oz of sugar per week in lieu of gruel for breakfast, if deemed expedient to make this change.
CHILDREN under 9 years of age to be dieted as discretion; - above 9 to be allowed same quantities as women.
SICK to be dieted as directed by Medical Officer.

Officially recommended diet for workhouse inmates

The annual treat for the inmates of Bolton and Turton workhouses took place on Christmas Day 1859, when they were regaled with a dinner after the good old English custom of roast beef and plum pudding served in the school room, which was handsomely decorated. The Guardians and Union officers dropped in during the day. Some of the residents in the neighbourhood also paid a casual visit. The thanks of the poor people was conveyed to the Board, and also to the Master and Matron, Mr & Mrs Brooks. Through the liberality of the Board Chairman, J Winder Esq., oranges were supplied to the inmates.

The dark and rat-infested dead-house at Turton was loathed by all and not only corpses were kept in it. During 1859 and 1860 it was reported that naughty boys were confined to the dead-house for offences such as talking during meals, stealing, and throwing stones. Some offenders were bound with rope and hanged off their feet with a weight tied to them as a punishment. Lighter punishment consisted of being beaten with a rope.

4.5 The Farm

The farm buildings had a chequered history from the start having had several tenants and uses. Although the Guardians of the Bolton Union became tenants of the principal workhouse buildings from 1839, the farm buildings, stock and adjacent land were not included. A public notice appeared on the 22 April 1844 related to a meeting for letting Goose Cote Hill Farm. The lot was described as a good farm house, barn and outbuildings, and 8 acres of good meadow and pasture land of large measure. The letting meeting was held at Turton Workhouse on Saturday 4 May 1844.

In 1847 more interest started to be taken in the farm, as a means of providing labour for the unemployed poor, and a deputation of the Board of Guardians was appointed to negotiate with its owner and occupier. By February 1854 there was concern about the inadequate provision for Turton's sick poor, and it was thought the farm building might be sufficiently roomy to hospitalise them. There were also a large number of boys in the workhouse who could be trained to work on the farm land. In May 1854 the Bolton Guardians became the tenants to the trustees of the farm and land for 7 years at an annual rent of £30 for the first 3 years and £40 p.a. thereafter. In November 1854 it was recommended that the farmhouse be adapted into a suitable place for the reception of insane persons and the accommodation of children with scarlet fever. By 1860, the farm, cattle and stock had been recommended for closure and disposal; milk, butter and potatoes having been provided by the farm which employed a dairy maid.

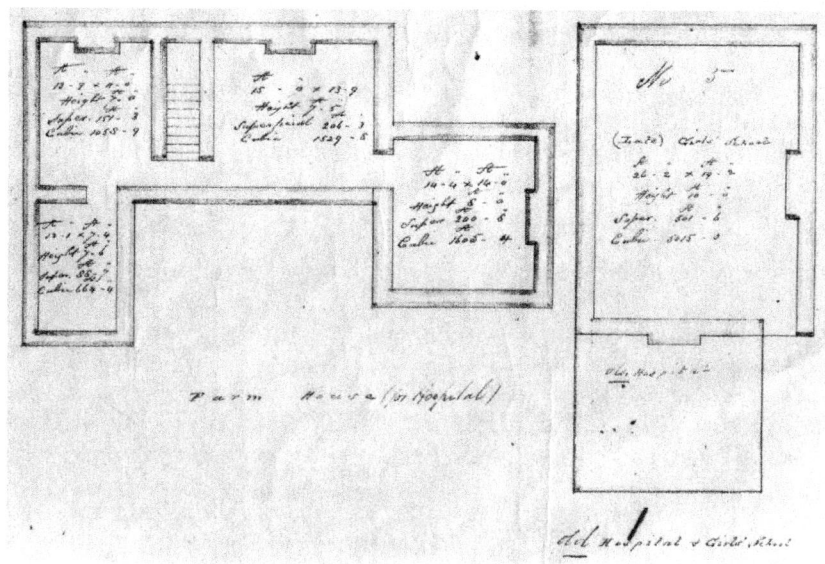

Plan of the Farmhouse showing accommodation for girls and boys.

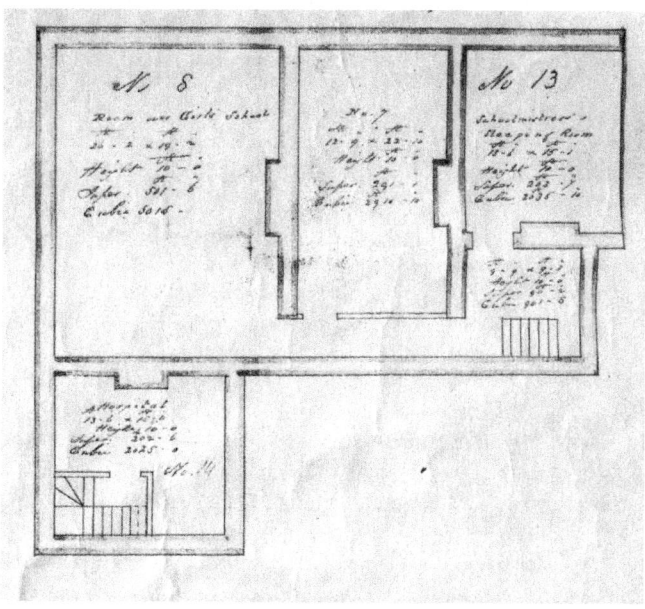

Plan of Old Hospital. Data on each room's height, dimensions, area and volume are included in both upper and lower plans: c1854.

4.6 Education

Education matters at Turton Workhouse were well discussed at various levels between 1851 and 1854. Poor Law legislation, the Poor Law Inspectors (Mr. Manwaring and later Mr. Farnall), and Her Majesty's Inspector of Schools (Mr. Browne) all influenced the future of workhouse education at Turton.

During March 1851 the Committee, having inspected the workhouse children, recommended that 14 boys aged 7-13 and 5 girls aged 8-11 be sent to the Swinton Industrial School. The Poor Law at that time prevented this, but the necessary change was made a few months later. In May 1851 an HMI of Schools reported: *'The children of this workhouse (Turton) passed a very unsatisfactory examination, more especially the girls who could scarcely answer any question. The boys do not appear accustomed to think or give their minds to what they are about. The state of education in this Union is deplorable'*

Initially, the Poor Law Inspector would not sanction the converting of Turton Workhouse into a school for pauper children from Bolton and Turton. Much concern was expressed that children were being brought up to pauperism and might be expected to become a permanent charge on the parochial funds instead of being trained so they might be able to earn a livelihood when they grew up. Children in the workhouse with adults observed idle habits and might grow up to be persons with similar traits.

During the following few months, nothing was done to improve education at Turton as it was thought advisable to postpone further consideration until the Guardians had decided about the erection of a new Union workhouse. In the meantime, Turton children would continue to be sent to the National School at Walmsley. This was supported and encouraged by the Committee of Privy Council on Education, whose Board nominated Mr Browne to the office of inspector. The Vicar of Walmsley, the Rev'd John Richardson, suggested that any examination of children's education would be better done at the National School by its school master, rather than in the confines of the workhouse.

In February 1852 some members of the workhouse committee were perfectly satisfied with the answers given by the children to Mr Browne's examination, even though he asked some difficult questions. But Mr Browne maintained that their education was not adequate for them to be emancipated from pauperism. He recommended the appointment of a schoolmaster and schoolmistress for all the children in the Union and estimated that the cost of educating children at Turton would be less than at Swinton. Costs would be 3s-3d per head per week at Swinton but only about 2s at Turton, a saving of around £125 per year. Also, alterations would have to be made to Turton Workhouse to make it suitable for use as a school.

In September 1852 plans and estimates for converting the workhouse into a school with residence for staff were forwarded to the PLB. Permission was sought and given for fitting up the school with desks, seating, fixtures, books, slates etc.

The 1834 Poor Law Act required education in numeracy and literacy to be given for three hours a day to the children and a schoolmaster to be employed by each Board of Guardians. The first government grant towards workhouse teachers' salaries was made in 1846. In December 1852 the PLB expressed an interest in workhouse school certification and parliamentary grants towards the salaries of schoolmasters and schoolmistresses. Forms were to be completed as soon as the schoolmaster and schoolmistress were appointed at Turton.

Advertisements for teachers were made in Bolton and Manchester newspapers and repeated until enough applications were received. Applicants who did not produce testimonials in accordance with the advertisement were rejected. No travelling or expenses for interviews were allowed. In January 1852 there were 7 applicants for the post of schoolmaster and Mr Charles Hall of Manchester was appointed. He was formerly a pupil at the Educational College, Chester, for 12 months and afterwards a schoolmaster at Bennett Street School, Manchester before his appointment to Turton Workhouse. Of 3 applicants in 1852 for the post of schoolmistress, Mrs Sarah Stewart of Manchester was appointed.

An extract from the Bolton Guardians report dated 8 February 1854 reads: *'Your Committee have to report with reference to the manner in which Mr Charles Hall the schoolmaster has performed the duties of his office during the past 6 months, that they are unanimously of the opinion that he has conducted the school satisfactorily and that he is in every respect a very suitable person for the situation he now holds, they are more convinced in this opinion on account of his examination by HMIs of Schools, some little time since, having resulted in his obtaining a certificate of probation from the Committee of Council on Education which will entitle the Guardians to £25 pa in part reimbursement of his salary.'*

In February 1856 Mrs Stewart asked for a testimonial to apply for a position at Wortley School near Sheffield. The guardians gave her a glowing report enthusing that: *'if she should succeed in obtaining the job, the Wortley Guardians would secure the services of a very experienced and efficient teacher and one well qualified in every respect to fill the situation of schoolmistress.'* Mrs Stewart resigned her appointment at Turton in September 1856. The workhouse committee produced a report regarding her replacement and the PLB wanted to know the reason for her resignation.

On the 19 March 1857 a probation certificate was awarded to Mr Hall. His teaching skills were described as *'fair'* and the state of his school *'pretty fair'*. The average number of pupils under his care was 50. A later school inspection gave him a certificate of competency *'2nd Division, state of school improved, skill as a teacher good'*. The average number of pupils was 41. A certificate was awarded to Mr Hall by the Council for Education on 25 March 1857, which entitled the Guardians to a payment of £30 in respect of his salary for the year.

During the following year the Guardians gave Mr Hall permission to reside outside the workhouse and agreed to 14 days leave of absence from his duties for *'recreation'*. During August 1859 the Guardians received a letter from Mr Hall intimating that he intended to apply for the office of Relieving Officer in Leigh Union and asked for a testimonial. However Mr Hall did not move to Leigh as, in November 1859, the Committee of Council for Education issued a certificate entitling the Bolton Guardians to claim from the government on Mr Hall's behalf £35 for the year ending Lady Day 1860.

Mr Hall moved to Fishpool Workhouse in 1861 as schoolmaster at the age of 32 at a salary of £60pa. He had to apply for his job there even though he was already in post at Turton. He was married with one child and he intended that his wife and child should reside with him in the workhouse. But the PLB would not agree, as they were neither officers nor inmates and therefore subject to *'no discipline'*. So Mr Hall was allowed to become a non-resident and to live outside with his family. He died from *'fever'* in April 1874.

4.7 Accommodation

The workhouse master in December 1854 was James Aitken and Catherine Booth was the house servant. A statement of the money spent on alterations and improvements was £1141-19s-6d up to 25 March 1855. The Guardians by this time felt it would be wiser to spend money on a new establishment. Much discussion took place regarding a new larger workhouse for the whole Union.

A PLB circular received on 28 March 1855 asked for the number of children registered and how much space was allowed to each inmate. Mr Robinson, the Medical Officer, said 8 cubic yards had been allowed. He described the isolated position of the workhouse and said that nearly all the inmates were children of 7-8 years average age. He considered the amount of cubic space to be sufficient. However, on the 2 May following, the PLB asked for confirmation of the measurements of the rooms concerned, to which Mr Robinson responded.

A PLB letter of July 1855 fixed 105 as the largest number of paupers to be housed at any one time including hospital accommodation at the farmhouse. A statement was also enclosed giving the number of inmates to be accommodated in the several sleeping wards and requesting that this practise may be carefully attended to. A PLB letter dated

18 July 1855 objected to the removal of the idiots from Bolton Workhouse to the farm at Turton as it appeared from their Inspector's report that the premises were not adapted for that type of pauper.

A letter to the Guardians of 14 August 1855 said they had received a communication from the Master asking how he should reduce the number of inmates to the limit fixed by the Board. Mr Aitken advised that it would be best for him not to receive anyone until the limit was attained. He also requested that the Guardians consider if other measures could be used to immediately reduce the number of paupers in the workhouse. A letter from Mr H B Farnall, the PLB Inspector, was read the following month asking how many children were in the workhouse, if they still exceeded the number fixed by the PLB and what steps the Guardians were taking to reduce numbers to the limit.

Bolton Union Committee on 26 December 1855 agreed to improve and enlarge Turton Workhouse. This was at a time when Bolton Workhouse was full with 353 inmates, the limit set by the PLB. The shortage of workhouse places meant that the Relieving Officer was regularly approached to arrange outdoor relief.

The salary paid to James Aitken, the Turton Master in 1855, for the quarter ending 25 March, 1855 was £13-15s-0d. Charles Hall's salary during the same period was £15-0s-0d, and the school mistress drew a salary of £7-5s-0d. Other salaries were £1-19s-0d for the house servant, and £16-5s-0d for the doctor. Following the resignation of Mr Aitken, Mr Frederick Brooks and Mrs Brooks were appointed Master and Matron in December 1855.

In February 1856 the Guardians applied to the PLB for an increase to the limit of inmates from 150 to 170 in Turton Workhouse. This was at a time of great hardship in the cotton trade with mills shut down or on short time. But the PLB objected to any departure from the specified number. During 1857 plans were produced to alter the farmhouse accommodation.

More changes at the Workhouse took place in April 1859. The clerk produced a statement on capacity with the numbers that each room would accommodate. The document, signed by the Medical Officer, was intended to allow an increase in the number of inmates beyond the limit set by the PLB, following the removal of the girls to Bolton Workhouse. The Board approved of the numbers suggested by the medical officer and ordered that the statement be sent to the PLB. During the following November the chairman produced a ground plan of the sleeping rooms and a statement on the sizes in cubic feet made by Mr Greenhalgh, the architect. This was forwarded to the PLB and a limit recommended of 165 occupants. In February a letter from the PLB was received consenting to the increase to 165 in the number to be accommodated at any one time.

Statement of Room Capacities, April 1859.

Class of Inmate	Day use or Night	L	B	H	Cu Ft	No
Men	day	22	16	8	2816	
Boys	day	22	15	8	2640	
Women	day	18	14	8	2016	
Boys' schoolroom	day	43	22	9	8514	
Young children in lower room*	day	15	12	10	1800	
Boys	night	26	19	9	4446	15
Women	night	15	13	10	1950	6
Women	night	23	12	10	2760	9
Women	night	26	19	10	4800	17
Men	night	28	18	8	4032	13
Children	night	22	16	8	2816	9
Men and Boys **	night	55	12	8	5280	32
Young children in upper room*	night	15	12	10	1800	6

Old farmhouse to be used as a hospital

Lower rooms	day	14	14	7	1372	3
		17	13	7	1365	3
Upper rooms	day	14	14	8	1568	3
	day	15	13	7	1365	3
	day	14	11	7	1078	2
	day	12	7	7	588	1

L = Length, B = Breath, H = Height.
* = At old hospital. ** = In stud partition rooms
No = Number of inmates the room will accommodate in the opinion of the Medical Officer. In this column the PLB changed 17 women to 16, 32 men and boys to 18 and the number in the larger upper room from 3 to 4.

Between June 1857 and April 1858 the men's day room floor was flagged by Orrell Holt of Entwistle, also some whitewashing and glazing work was carried out. In May 1859 estimates from Jonathan Leach and James Brooks for whitewashing were laid before the Board and that from James Brooks for £5-10s-0d was accepted. Two months later, it was ordered that the exterior of the workhouse be whitewashed where needed.

However, in January 1856, the Bolton Board of Guardians had started to negotiate to buy 8 statute acres of land in Farnworth known as Fishpool Farm. The land was purchased in 1858 and a corner stone laid for the new workhouse which was completed in September 1861. Paupers from Bolton and Turton were then sent to *'Fishpool'* and existing inmates at Fletcher Street and Turton workhouses transferred there. Turton Workhouse then became redundant.

4.8 Health and Medical Matters

Under the 1834 Act a qualified medical officer was required to attend to the sick, but nursing was often carried out by untrained female inmates and for some time, little in the way of medical help was provided by the PLGs. Where large groups of enclosed people were not allowed out, infectious diseases spread like wildfire and tuberculosis was rife in many workhouses. At Turton Workhouse in July 1847 chloride of zinc was recommended as a disinfectant to be used on people or premises. In May 1848 smallpox was prevalent and much attention was given to the vaccination of inmates.

Even when Unions had appointed medical officers, rates of pay which included the provision of medicine were scarcely sufficient to cover adequate treatment. Also, people had little confidence in *'parish doctors'* and their drugs. Whenever possible, poor families preferred to seek assistance from dispensaries, where they felt they received better attention and superior medicine, but there were many who could not reach a dispensary and whose children died for lack of medical aid.

In due course, more provision was made for the destitute sick in infirmaries although these institutions were often shunned because they were identified with the socially outcast. There were lying-in wards where a large proportion of births were illegitimate and where the death rate of such unfortunate infants was high. So great was the stigma attached to birth in a workhouse that there were families who pawned all they had to avoid it.

In August 1848 the Bolton Guardians were informed by Mr James Pendlebury the medical officer, of a female inmate sick with fever for whom there was not proper accommodation. Six years later, the medical officer attended the PLB and informed it there were 15 cases of scarlet fever among Turton's workhouse children and no accommodation provided for their proper treatment. He recommended that the Board should allow the upper part of the farmhouse to be used for the reception and accommodation of these children, which was agreed.

In 1851 two boys, classed as idiots and subject to fits of epilepsy, were ordered to be removed from Turton Workhouse to Bolton Workhouse. It was ordered in November 1854 that a committee be appointed to supervise the conversion of the farmhouse at Turton into a suitable place for the reception of idiots and insane persons from Bolton Union who were then confined in the County Lunatic Asylums and whose habits were not of a dangerous or violent character. The committee consisted of Messrs: Best, Longworth, Hodson, Green, Nicholson and Hubbersty. The following July Mr Robinson had examined the farmhouse and considered it would accommodate 16 of the insane from Bolton Workhouse. A wall having been built and alterations made for their reception, PLB approval was sought. In April 1854 an account from the Prestwich

Lunatic Asylum for £104-5s owing for the maintenance of pauper lunatics belonging to the Bolton Union was ordered to be paid.

A committee discussion in 1852 considered the health of the children. Mr Barrow, a committee member, said the food which the children consumed was not of sufficient solidity and that their appearance was such that when at school they might easily be singled out. Mr Latham, chairman, said the schoolmaster had pointed out habits of the children which showed that their food must be of too sloppy a character. Mr Ashworth said it was not to be expected that these workhouse children would look like farmers' children. He wished however to ask Mr Lowe if the medical officer had not given favourable testimony as to their condition. Mr Lowe said the medical officer had stated that he had never seen healthier children. He (Mr Lowe) thought they were as healthy as most other Guardians' children and they had sufficient food. Mr Latham begged to say that they had not had sufficient on New Year's Day. The chairman said the Guardians might, if they saw fit, alter the diet and make it more solid. On the motion of Mr Winder it was agreed that the subject should be enquired into by the Workhouse Committee. It was noted in the medical officer's brief in March 1853 that the effects of pea soup appeared to be too purging for the children.

On September 8th 1852 the medical officer reported to the Board of Guardians the following statement: *'That since the PLB fixed the number of adults to be admitted into Turton Workhouse an enlargement of the premises was made which is now exclusively appropriated for children. In his opinion there was at present ample sleeping room for upwards of 160 children provided small iron bedsteads were substituted for many of the wood ones now in use. If the proposed alterations were made for a school, the house would still be adequate to accommodate 150 children.'* The PLB was requested to sanction the same and fixed the number of children at 150. In November 1852 the medical officer felt it his duty to report the immediate necessity of doing away with the dangerous practice of drying clothes in the day rooms, as one old woman, Sarah Hughes, *'was occasioned by the severe and dangerous case of Bronchitis'*.

The medical officer stated in February 1854 that the present sick hospital was very inadequate and it would be found to be more so should the workhouse be visited by any epidemic or contagious disease, against which at all times adequate accommodation should be in readiness. There were 146 paupers in Turton Workhouse in April 1854 and reports were made about the unhealthy state of the children with 45 sick on the doctor's book. Skin disease was prevalent, the water quality being blamed. The Medical officer Mr Robinson stated that the hospital accommodation should be at least doubled if skin problems were to be improved. He had examined the farmhouse on the land the Guardians proposed to take and considered it would make an excellent hospital.

Workhouse children often had scrofulous glands and inflamed eyes. Sore eyes, the result of malnutrition, were the particular mark of the workhouse, where child's eyelids might be covered with scabs and scales. During February 1856 the Chairman read a communication from Manchester Eye Hospital on William Collins and Hannah Rigby of Bolton Union and inmates of the hospital. Both were undergoing treatment for eye disease at the hospital and improving as well as could be expected. The house surgeon, Mr John Morris, monitored Hannah's progress over the following weeks and considered discharging her for *'a change of air'* but eventually decided to let her remain in hospital until her health improved. Three months later, William Connell an eye hospital patient from the workhouse, was well enough to be discharged and returned to the workhouse.

Commonly, workhouse children suffered from infested heads and from scabies, a disease known as the *'itch'*. Even the old institutions were compelled to set-up boys' itch wards (girls were usually put in with women). Ringworm, associated with fungal growth at the hair roots and scalphead, where the scalp was encrusted with sores and scabs, were the hardest head conditions to eradicate. An incident occurred at Turton Workhouse in March 1858 when the medical officer complained that a family had recently been sent to the workhouse by the relieving officer Mr Rothwell, some of whom were afflicted with itch and that no wards were provided for the treatment of such cases. He also pointed out the danger of children with itch coming into contact with the rest of the inmates.

4.9 Religion

It was made clear in 1834 that no inmate was to be obliged to attend any religious service contrary to his principles or have his children educated against his wishes. Dissenting ministers were to have the right of attending when requested by an inmate. The Rev'd William Probert, of Walmsley Unitarian Chapel, regularly baptised and buried people from Goose Cote Hill and the Methodists held services there from 1818. During August 1844 the Workhouse Committee was asked to provide, at the cost of the Union, a sufficient quantity of Bibles and Testaments for the use of the inmates of both workhouses.

In 1853 the Rev'd E Carter called attention to the difficulty for Catholics if all the children were placed in Turton Workhouse and educated there, as the nearest Catholic Chapel was in Little Bolton. He suggested that Catholic children should be in Bolton Workhouse and offered to educate them free in a Catholic School. There was much discussion on this matter, particularly as the Catholic children would lose out on the industrial training provided at Turton and a rearrangement of the Bolton Workhouse would be necessary. After further discussion it was decided to keep all the children at Turton where ministers of any denomination would be able to visit and instruct them in the faith of their parents.

4.10   Equipment

A list of items purchased by the committee in 1842 to 1859 is as follows:

DATE		SUPPLIER	ITEMS	COST		
				£	s	d
Apr	1851	Sara James	Brooms	4	8	0
Sept	1852	Benjamin Abbot	Mop rags	2	2	6
Sept	1852	James Moscrop	*Bed ticking	2	9	10
Oct	1852	William Hinks	*Trencher	1	6	6
Oct	1852	William Coop	Spoons		2	0
Oct	1852	James Haworth	Iron bedsteads	7	15	0
Mar	1855	Joseph Lowe	Soft soap etc	2	2	10
July	1855	William Worsley	Squeezer repairs		18	0
Mar	1856	James Morris	Paint		18	3
Mar	1856	Peter Higson	Castors		7	0
Mar	1856	Constantine Bros	Carpeting	6	2	0
Mar	1856	James West	New clock and clock repairs	4	0	0
Mar	1856	Rigby & Co	Iron plates for stove	1	15	0
Apr	1856	Henry Higson	bedsteads	35	11	6
Apr	1856	Henry Higson	fireguard	1	5	9
May	1857	Pickley & Co	Bedsteads	17	6	6
May	1857	W Mulligan	Cupboard	3	0	0
Nov	1858	Thomas Thwaites	Boiler		12	6
Jan	1859	William Coop	Spectacles		1	0

* Bed ticking is a mattress. A trencher is a wooden plate.

Other items included: squeezers for clothes, second-hand mangle, boiler, soap, black lead, drying stove, dubbing, straw, candles, thimbles, needles, buckets, starch, washing crystals, weighing machine, washing liquor and utensils, matting, water taps, smoothing iron, blue smalt (silica, potash and cobalt), 2 coal boxes, 4 floor scopes (mops), 6 dolly tubs and 12 washing tubs. Kitchen items included: 7 dishes, 24 plates, 6 breakfast cups and saucers, 6 common basins, 6 pint and 2 large milk jugs, 4 washing-up tins, 1 slop can, 1 teapot.

4.11   Ongoing Problems

Although Bolton's Fishpool Workhouse accommodated Turton's paupers from the 1860s, there were still problems in the community in Turton. The case of a certified lunatic, Michael Hullock, makes interesting reading. An order signed by the parish curate and the relieving officer of Turton District and the superintendent of the County Asylum on 17 March 1868 committed Michael to Prestwich Asylum. The medical certificate signed by the surgeon states Michael sat in silence from morning till night. He imagined he was in communion with a spiritual being, who instructed him to conduct himself so. He died ten years later on the 19 March 1878 at Prestwich. Michael's brother, Adam, a 19 years old quarryman of Dimple Row, being a person certified of unsound mind, was also sent to Prestwich Asylum on 7 March, 1874. The order was signed by the Incumbent of Walmsley, the Rev'd R C W Croft and the Relieving Officer for the Turton District of the Bolton Union, Jonathan Carrodus. He was admitted on 9 March 1874 by the Asylum's superintendent but soon recovered after care and treatment and left on the 20 April 1874.

Order for receiving patients into Prestwich Asylum.

Statement.

If any Particulars in this Statement be not known, the Fact to be stated.

Name of Patient, and Christian Name at length	Michael Hullock
Sex and Age	Male – 20 years
Married, Single, or Widowed	Single
Condition of Life, and Previous Occupation (if any)	Factory Operative
The Religious Persuasion, as far as known	Church of England
Previous Place of Abode	Bolton Workhouse
Whether First Attack	Yes
Age (if known) on First Attack	20 years
When and where previously under care and Treatment	Bolton Workhouse
Duration of existing Attack	Nine Months
Supposed Cause	Not Known
Whether subject to Epilepsy	No
Whether Suicidal	Yes
Whether Dangerous to others	No
Parish or Union to which the Lunatic is chargeable	Common Fund of the Bolton Union
Name and Christian Name, and Place of abode of nearest known Relative of the Patient, and Degree of Relationship, if known	Margaret Hullock, Mason Row, Turton, his Mother

I certify that, to the best of my knowledge, the above Particulars are correctly stated.

Signed, Name, (1) Jonathan Carrodus, Relieving Officer, Turton District, Bolton Union.

(1) Relieving officer or overseer.

Statement for admission to Prestwich Asylum.

GOOSE COTE HILL FARM.
TO BE LET,
BY TICKET,

On SATURDAY, the 4th day of May next,

At Six o'clock in the Evening,

At the WORKHOUSE, in TURTON,
ALL THAT

FARM,
Called Goose Cote Hill,

Consisting of a good Farm House, Barn, and Outbuildings, and Eight Acres of good Meadow and Pasture Land, of the large measure. The above Farm is well situated and near good roads.

For further particulars apply to *THOS. WOOD*, Farmer, or *JOHN ASHWORTH, Jun.*, Land Agent, both of *Turton*.

TURTON, APRIL 22nd, 1844.   [Gardner, Printer, Bolton.]

Advertisement for letting Goose Cote Hill Farm, 1844.

The Sportsmans Arms where the 1863 auction
of the old Turton Workhouse took place.

CHAPTER V   CLOSURE, PUBLIC HOUSE AND DEMOLITION

5.1   Closure and Sale

The 1861 census showed 104 residents in Turton Workhouse, including the Master and Matron, one servant and 101 inmates, 43 of the latter being scholars. The master was John Taylor, 45, and born in Little Bolton; his wife Ellen, 43, born in Henley-on-Thames and the servant Alice Whewell, 45, born in Tyldesley. The inmates were mostly born in Bolton Parish with a few from elsewhere in Lancashire or further afield as follows: 42 from Great Bolton, 14 Little Bolton, 4 Turton, 1 Edgworth, 1 Sharples, 1 Longworth, 1 Tockholes, 1 Breightmet, 1 Halliwell, 3 Heaton, 1 Great Lever, 1 Horwich, 1 Lostock, 3 Westhoughton, 1 Middle Hulton, 1 Rumworth, 1 Farnworth, 1 Rochdale, 1 Whittle, 1 Coppice, 1 Croston, 1 Wigan, 1 Preston, 1 Swinton, 1 Oldham, 1 Salford, 1 Manchester, 2 Liverpool, 2 Yorkshire, 1 London, 7 Ireland and 1 Scotland.

When the new Fishpool Workhouse was opened on the 28 September 1861 and Turton's inmates were moved there, the Turton premises became redundant and remained closed until 1863. The 1871 census gives the total number of residents in Bolton Workhouse (Fishpool) as 366.

As trustees of the Humphrey Chetham's Charity, Henry and John Ashworth, called a Vestry Meeting of rate payers and property owners in Turton to dispose of the old workhouse. They intended to convert it to a factory or the like. Otherwise it was thought the whole of the premises might be sold for building materials to the highest bidder.

Following the appearance of a press advertisement in 1862 an enquiry was made by Bury Solicitor William Harper, acting on instructions from Canon Edmund Carter of SS Peter & Paul's Church, Bolton and of the Roman Catholic Diocese of Salford, about purchasing the premises for a Roman Catholic boys' reformatory school.

Harper enquired about a fixed rent lease for seven years with an option to buy at any time. After a meeting of the trustees and township rate payers at the workhouse on 16 January 1863, their solicitor Mr R. Winder replied to Mr Harper that the ratepayers showed themselves disinclined to allow use of the premises for a reformatory school, but would negotiate as there were no other offers.

Further negotiations then took place. Winder duly offered the premises to Harper at an annual rent of £100 pa for a term of say 21 years, with an option of purchase at the end of 23 years. But Harper's clients only offered £70 pa for a 21 year lease and a price of

TURTON WORKHOUSE.—GOOSE-COAT HILL.

THE Trustees of Chetham's Charity are Prepared to TREAT with any Person desirous of PURCHASING these BUILDINGS, to be Converted into Manufacturing or other purposes, subject to a reasonable chief rent to be agreed upon.

Or they are Prepared to SELL the whole of the said PREMISES for Building Materials to the highest bidder.

For further particulars apply to Mr. THOMAS DAWSON, Town Hall, Little Bolton; or to JOHN ASHWORTH, Esq., Rose-hill House, Turton.

24th April, 1862.

Notice of the sale of Turton Workhouse in 1862.

TO BE SOLD BY AUCTION,

By Mr. WILLIAM LOMAX, Jun., at the house of Mr JAMES KNOWLES, the SPORTSMAN'S ARMS INN, at Toppings, in Turton, in the county of Lancaster, on WEDNESDAY, the 26th day of August, 1863, at Six o'clock in the Evening, subject to such conditions as shall be then produced:

LOT 1. ALL those Two Freehold PLOTS OF LAND, situate at Goose Cote Hill, in Turton aforesaid, and the several Stone Buildings and other erections, comprising a capital Building three storeys high, with a frontage of upwards of 75 feet; another Building two storeys high, with a frontage of 40 feet; and a Cottage and other Outbuildings, with the yards and appurtenances thereto.

One of the Plots is now used as a garden, and the entire premises contain, including the site of the buildings, 2820 superficial square yards of land or thereabouts, and were formerly occupied by the Poor-law Guardians of the Bolton Union.

The main buildings could at a small cost be converted into a large and convenient Dwelling-house, and the vacant land is well adapted for the erection of respectable residences, being approached from the road by a gradual incline, and commanding an extensive view of the surrounding country.

Lot 2. A Freehold PLOT OF LAND, situate on the north westerly side of and adjoining to the last lot, with the two stone Buildings erected thereon, and containing, including the site of the buildings, 612 superficial square yards or thereabouts.

The buildings comprised in this lot could, at a very small outlay, be converted into five dwelling-houses.

For further particulars apply to Messrs. RUSHTON and ARMITSTEAD, Solicitors, Bolton, at whose offices a plan of the premises may be seen.

Notice for the 1863 auction of Turton Workhouse premises.

Map showing the new Bolton Union Workhouse at Fishpool, Farnworth, 1891.

The Bolton Union Workhouse at Fishpool when newly opened.

£1500. Harper was then asked for £80 pa over 21 years and a price of £1680 during or immediately after lease.

In the meantime James Kay of Turton Tower had offered £1600 for the estate, which the trustees thought was a firm offer and went on to consult with the Charity Commissioners for England & Wales. The Commissioners required a valuation of the property to be made by a competent person and Mr Piggot, a Bolton land agent and surveyor to the Earl of Bradford was retained. His report was such that the Commissioners refused Mr Kay's offer unless he increased it to £1700, which he eventually did, and which was accepted by the trustees and sanctioned by the Commissioners. The sale was transacted at an auction at the Sportsmans Arms Inn, Toppings on 26 August 1863.

Subsequently the trustees informed Mr Harper about the acceptance of Kay's offer, but by then Harper had written to the trustees accepting their offer after consultation with Dr William Turner, RC Bishop of Salford. The trustees were therefore obliged to pay £15 in compensation for legal fees to Mr Harper.

The purchase money was paid in cash by James Kay on 15 July 1863. The transaction included the whole estate including the farmhouse, the disused workhouse and 18 acres 2r 10p of land (probably Cheshire Measure). Trustee John Ashworth, resident at Rose Hill, retained copies of the correspondence and documents relating to the sale and subsequent investment of the money in 3% Government Securities. The income received from the investment was higher than the rent previously received from the workhouse and was used to buy cloth for 'doles' (charitable gifts of food, money and clothing).

During this period 'doles' were distributed by the overseers to deserving classes of people. In some places the overseers received a yearly sum from a charity to purchase cloth and then distributed it to the needy. A cloth consisted of either a blanket, a pair of sheets, 8 yds of calico, or 6 yds of flannel. The Turton trustees bought, generally in Bolton, calico, flannel, blankets and sheets and made a distribution twice annually in May and December. Records were kept but persons desiring a 'dole' had to make a fresh application on each occasion. The recipients' circumstances were investigated by a visitor who was paid £5 yearly. Those qualified and accepted for 'doles' were neither in receipt of Poor Law Relief, nor had family members with average earnings exceeding 5 shillings per week. Single blankets (worth 6 shillings each) were normally issued, with doubles occasionally for the elderly. No more than one blanket was given every 3 years and the cloth was marked with the name of the charity to prevent improper use.

In January 1867 application to the Charity Commissioners was made by Henry Ashworth and John Ashworth, the surviving trustees of the Charity, that they might be discharged from the Trust and new trustees appointed. Notice was then given of the Commissioners' intent to appoint new trustees in the usual manner. Subsequently Henry and John Ashworth were removed from the trust and replaced with George Binns Ashworth of Birtenshaw, Edmund Naish Ashworth of Rose Hill and James Kay of Turton Tower, all from the township of Turton, together with William Slater of The Holmes in Little Bolton. The new trustees, who had already signified their willingness to accept, were duly appointed to administer the charity. Their powers included *'the right to sue for, recover, and receive; and give receipts and discharges for all sums of money and choices in action due to or recoverable for the benefit of the said charity'*. They were appointed on 28 August 1867 under the common seal of the Commissioners.

5.2 The Beerhouse

Between 1863 and 1866 James Kay sold some of the Goose Cote Hill property to Richard Rainham Rothwell of Sharples Hall, Bolton. The former three-storey workhouse building became known as the De Rothwell Arms, Cox Green, a house licensed to sell beer, which was probably brewed on the premises.

On Wednesday 15 July 1891 the freehold beer house and bowling green, then owned by Richard Rothwell, was auctioned as:

Lot 2: *'The De Rothwell Arms, Cox Green Road, presently occupied by Mrs Alice Haslam, beer seller, together with three adjoining stone-built cottages'*.

The existing tenancy was due to expire on the 25 December 1891, the site was freehold, free from chief rent, comprised 2613 square yards and was contiguous with the well known Cox Green Stone quarries. The auctioneers were Lomax, Sons & Mills and the solicitors were Holden & Holden.

Notice of sale of the De Rothwell Arms, 1891.

The De Rothwell Arms c1910: one of the very few surviving images of the old workhouse.

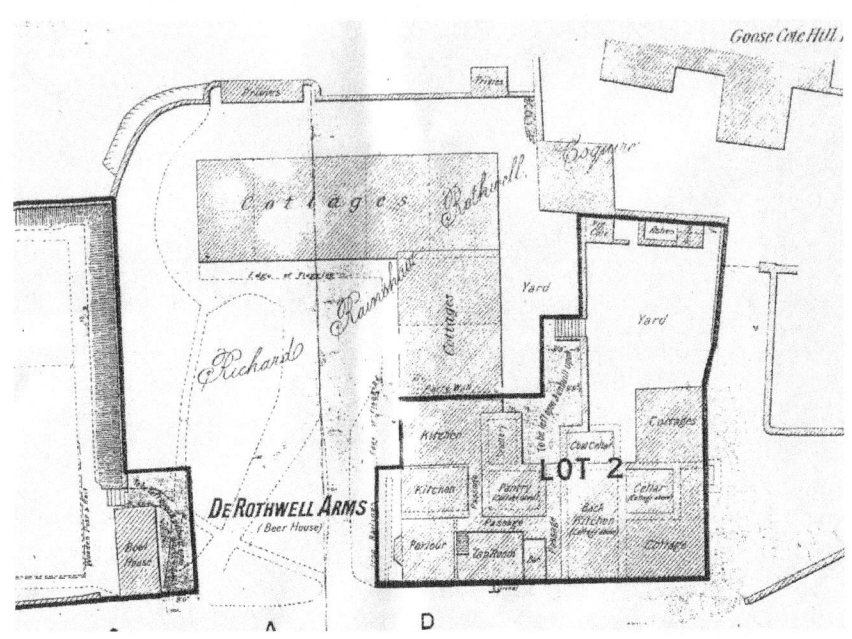

Plan of the De Rothwell Arms published in connection with its sale.

The former Turton Workhouse alongside Cox Green Quarry, c1920.

The Beer House was bought by Edward Halliwell of J Halliwell & Son, Alexandra Brewery, Mount Street, Bolton, for £480. Subsequently Halliwells were acquired by Magee Marshall & Co Ltd, Crown Brewery, Bolton in 1910. A change of ownership occurred in 1910 when the beer house was acquired by Duttons, Blackburn Brewery Co Ltd with Albert Nightingale as occupant and licensee.

During the period when the premises were functioning as a beerhouse the licensees included Sarah Scholes, R Scholes, Luke Haslam, William Bentley, James Haslam, Alice Haslam, Joe Mayoh, and Albert Nightingale.

During the early 1930s the building ceased to trade as a beerhouse and was converted to tenanted habitations known as Rothwell Cottages. The quarry, owned and worked by Walsh, had its problems when the men went on strike for higher wages in 1914. Phillipsons took it over and continued to work and expand the quarry. During the early 1940s, cottage residents were warned about quarry blasting by the hoisting of a clearly visible white flag after which the buildings would tremble. The old workhouse buildings by this time had been reduced to two storeys and were finally vacated in 1946 before the expanding quarry eliminated the site.

ALEXANDRA BREWERY,

MOUNT-STREET, BOLTON.

Proprietor · · · JOHN HALLIWELL.

FINE FAMILY

MILD AND STRONG ALES,

IN HALF BARRELS	XXX	26s.
IN QUARTER BARRELS	XXX	13s.
IN 18 GALLON CASKS	XX	20s.
IN 9 GALLON CASKS	XX	10s.

BITTER ALES,

IN 18 GALLON CASKS	26s.
IN 9 GALLON CASKS	13s.

Brewery advertisement.

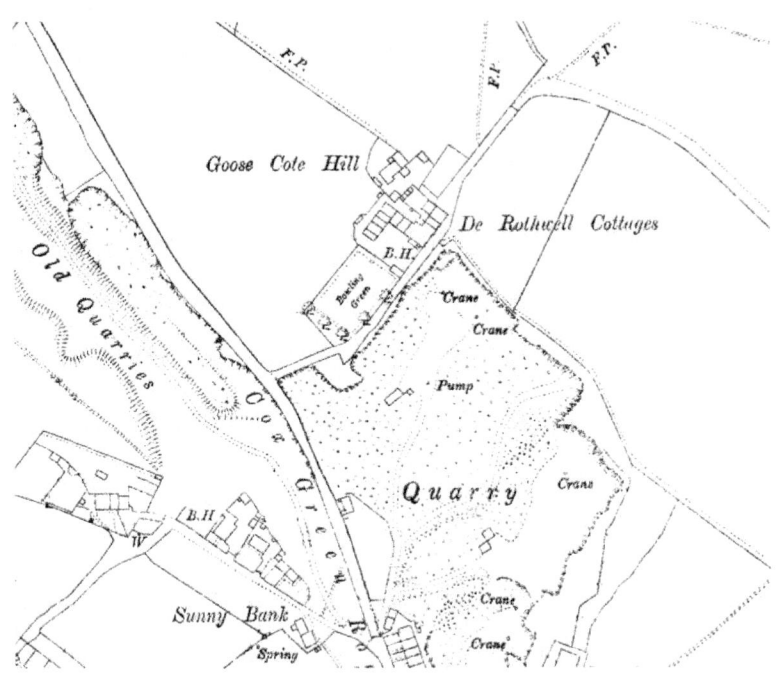

De Rothwell Cottages and Cox Green Quarry in the 1890s.

Members of Turton UDC Highways Committee inspecting a wall at Cox Green Quarry in 1946. The old workhouse building is in the background.

The workhouse site in 2011. The whole area was quarried away in the period 1946-1966 and the land surface lowered by about 10m. The workhouse was approximately situated above the left centre of the photograph.

Cox Green Road adjacent to Cox Green Quarry, 2009.

APPENDIX 1   TRUSTEES AND GOVERNORS

Humphrey Chetham Charity (HCC) Trustees

Around 1736 Samuel Chetham gave, for posterity, the Goose Cote Hill estate to the HCC Trustees, who included:

1.6. 1748	John Wilson, John Lomax
1.7.1748	John Nuttall, John Orrell, John Wood
7.8.1781	John Wood and John Orrell made agreement with Samuel Holt, Overseer of the Poor
19.7.1786	Isaac Orrell (son of John Orrell), John Ashworth
12.8.1823	Thomas Wood, John Ashworth (Jun.) Henry Ashworth.
28.8.1867	George B Ashworth, Edmund Naish Ashworth, James Kay, William Slater

Four more appointments were made on 2 May 1899 and three more on 29 Aug 1899 as follows:

G B Ashworth	Bromley Cross
Robert Ashworth	Windy Harbour, Land Agent
Wm Thos Dixon	High St Turton, Schoolmaster
John Hulme	Hough Lane, Coal Agent
Walter Haslam	Egerton, Cashier
Edward Deakin	Belmont, Bleacher
G H Ashworth	Bertinshaw, Manufacturer

Governors (Masters) and Matrons at Turton Workhouse

1818-1839 William & Dorothy Sharples
1841-51 Robert & Elizabeth Lowe
1853-1855 James & Mrs Aitken
1856-1859 Mr & Mrs Brooks
1859-1861 John & Ellen Taylor

Tenants at the workhouse farm

1795	John Lawe	1828-31	Helme Horrocks
1798	James Rothwell	1831-43	James Halton
1803	Henry Knowles	1844	Henry Bromeley
1816	James Horrocks	1854-61	Bolton Board of Guardians
1818-27	Edmund Horrocks		

APPENDIX 2   MAINTENANCE, BAPTISMS AND BURIALS

Summonses for maintenance involving inmates at Turton Workhouse

Date	Defendant	Complaint	Offence	How Disposed
Nov 1844	John Walsh	Sarah Bibby, Sharples	Bastardy	
Jan 1845	Andrew Entwistle	Ann Walker, Harwood	Bastardy	
Apr 1846	Richard Haslam	Emma Boardman	Bastardy	
1846	James Kay	Jane Holden	Bastardy	Order for 1/-
Jun 1846	William Entwistle	Esther Walsh	Bastardy	Order for 2/-
Feb 1847	Charles Kay	Mary Hindle, Quarlton	Bastardy	
Feb 1847	Charles Simm	Margaret Crompton, Ent*.	Bastardy	
Mar 1847	John Mayho	Charlotte Greenhalgh	Bastardy	
Aug 1847	James Yates	Ann Booth	Bastardy	
Jan 1852	Samuel Horrocks	Betty Bentley, Edgworth	Bastardy	2/- per week
Jan/Mar	John Rothwell	Jane Howard	Bastardy	2/- per week
Jan/Mar	Charles Simm	Margaret Crompton, Ent*.	Bastardy	2/- per week
1852	Ellis Hornby	Jane Entwistle	Bastardy	2/- per week
1852	George Banks	Mary Rooney	Bastardy	2/- per week
Mar 1853	Adam Helme	Hannah Rothwell	Bastardy	did not appear
Mar/Jun	Thomas Cooper	Sophia Mayoh	Bastardy	Dismissed
Sept 1853	Bannister Craws	Mary Horrocks, Tonge	Bastardy	2/- per week
Nov 1853	James Cooper	Hannah Mayoh	Bastardy	2/- per week
May 1854	Hargreaves Rad*	Martha Brogden, Sharples	Bastardy	
Jul 1854	Robert Horrocks	Mary Brooks, Tonge	Bastardy	
Aug 1854	Thomas Bury	Mary Kay	Bastardy	
Nov 1854	James Walsh	Alice Isherwood	Bastardy	
Apr 1855	John Rothwell	Mary Howard, Turton	Bastardy	
May 1855	Thomas Hulme	Elizabeth Redford?	Bastardy	
Jun 1855	Adam Brindle	Ann Mather	Bastardy	2/- per week
Jun 1855	Wm Wolfenden	Mary Smith	Bastardy	2/- per week
Jul 1856	Jepson Jepson	Nancy Fielding, Turton	Bastardy	
Oct 1856	Jeremiah Marsh	Esther Entwistle	Bastardy	2/6 per week
Oct 1856	William Simm	Sarah Hornby, Longworth	Bastardy	
Feb 1858	William Marsden	Jane Pilkington	Bastardy	Dismissed.
Feb 1858	James Crook	Alice Mather	Bastardy	2/- per week
Jul/Sep	Thomas Howarth	Ann Mather	Bastardy	1/6 per week

In the above table:
Ent* = Entwistle
Rad* = Radcliffe

Transcript from the Register of Baptisms at Walmsley Chapel involving inmates of Turton Workhouse 1784 to 1819.

Year	M	D	Surname	Childs Name	Born	Y	Father Name	Mother Name	Nee
1784	Oct	29	Bromily	William			William	Martha	
1787	Oct	3	Bromily	Isaac	Sept 26		John	Mary	
1787	Oct	3	Holt	William	Sep 30		James	Susan	Howarth
1790	Mar	14	Bromily	Alice	Mar 8		John	Mary	Entwistle
1790	Mar	14	Mayoh	Margaret	Jan 28	1	John	Alice	Carter
1790	Apr	18	Holt	Alice	Apr 13		James	Susan	Haworth
1790	Apr	18	Mather	Isaac	Apr 4		James	Betty	Knowles
1791	Jan	25	Bothwell	Richard	Nov 25	1	John	Rachel	Isherwood
1791	Jul	3	Mather	Margaret	Jun 3		James	Betty	Knowles
1792	Jan	4	Green	Joseph	Dec 6	17		Susan	
1792	Jan		Bromley	Joseph				Betty	
1792	Jul	14	Mather	Alice	Mar 26		William	Betty	Holt
1793	Jan	13	Bromily	Joseph	Jan 9	19		Betty	
1793	Feb	3	Bromily	Ann	Jan 29	1	John	Mary	Entwistle
1793	Mar	17	Sharrocks	Elizabeth	Sep 6	17	Roger	Alice	Platt
1798	Jan	7	Crook	Charlotte	Dec 23	1	Peter	Alice	Longworth
1798	Jun	17	Sharocks	Betty	Apr 10		Roger	Alice	Platt
1798	Sep	30	Bothwell	William	Sep 18		James		
1800	Jan	19	Bothwell	William	Jan 14		James	Alice	
1802	Jan	27	Bothwell	James	Dec 5	18			Latham
1804	Jun	6	Boardman	Catherine			Thomas	Jane	Whitner
1805	Mar	20	Haslam	Charles				Mary	
1806	Feb	4	Moscrop	Robert				Dolly	
1810	Apr	12	Partington	Isabella				Alice	
1810	Apr	28	Benyon	Ann				Elizabeth	
1810	Dec	22	Haslam	Charlotte				Mary	
1812	Feb	18	Martin	Robert	Jun 17	1		Phebe	
1812	Feb	18	Rostron	Robert	Mar 11	1		Martha	
1812	Feb	18	Hayes	William	Jun 8	18		Mary	
1813	Oct	6	*Smethurst	Esther			Nathaniel	Sarah	Grey
1814	May	1	*Green	Peter	Feb 12	1	Thos	Hannah	Mather
1814	Sep	14	*Pickering	Sarah	Aug 21		John	Mary Ann	How
1815	Mar	29	*Settle	John	Feb 19		John	Ann	Livesey
1817	May	4	Eastwood	William			William	Ann	Disley
1817	May	4	*Hamer	William			Samuel	Nelly	Isherwood
1817	May	4	*Woolsome	Harriet			Thomas	Alice	Greenhalgh
1817	May	4	*Martin	Robert			Richard	Ann	Holt
1817	Jun	22	*Nuttall	Thomas			John	Mary	Rainford
1818	Feb	8	Helm	Dolly			James	Betty	Holt
1819	Nov	7	Brown	Mary	Sep 20			Ellin	Brown
1819	Nov	7	Holcroft	Alice	Oct 24		William	Ann	Rushton

1 *   In the case of illegitimate births the father's surname is given followed by the mother's. Thus certain surnames (col 4) are given in full as: Smethurst/Grey, Green/Mather, Pickering/How, Settle/Livesey, Hamer/Isherwood, Woolsome/Greenhalgh, Martin/Holt, Nuttall/Rainford.

2   Column headed Y is the number of years previous to the entry date in which the birth occurred.

3   The 1784 entry concerns a baptism in the Old Chapel.

4   Residences are variously listed in the original register as: ' Turton Workhouse'; 'Poorhouse, Turton'; 'Workhouse, Goose Cote'; 'Goose Cote Hill'; 'Goose Carr Hill'; and 'Goose Cote Hill, Turton'.

Burials of Workhouse Inmates at Walmsley Chapel

Year	Date	Surname	Christian name	Age	Residence
1792	Aug 2	Green	Joseph	26 wks	Goose Cote Hill
1826	May 25	Mather	Richard	89	Turton Workhouse
1831	Jul 26	Holt	Thomas	79	Goosecar Hill
1832	Jan 23	Holt	Nanny	73	Turton Workhouse
1832	Apr 1	Pilling	Mally	23	Turton Workhouse
1836	Apr 7	Hornby	Wm(?)	85	Turton Workhouse
1838	May 20	Mayoh	Daniel	33	Goosecar Hill
1839	Oct 13	Dean	Margaret	40	Workhouse
1843	Apr 16	Kay	Elizabeth	14 mth	Goosecar Hill
1844	Nov 10	Mather	Hannah	64	Turton Workhouse
1861	Jun 12	Mayoh	John	83	Workhouse

Walmsley Chapel where the above inmates were buried.

APPENDIX 3   CENSUS RETURNS

1841 Census Return (partial) for the Bolton Union Workhouse at Turton

Surname	Christian Name	Sex	Age	Occupation
Staff				
Lowe	Robert	m	35	governor, weaver
Lowe	Elizabeth	f	40	matron
Inmates				
Rostron	Thomas	m	65	weaver
Riley	John	m	60	man servant
Marsh	Mary	f	40	female servant
Whitley	Mary	f	50	no calling
Husby	Margaret	f	60	charwoman
Holt	John	m	45	no calling
Wylde	James	m	60	weaver
Roscow	Thomas	m	65	weaver
Edge	Thomas	m	55	weaver
Howarth	William	m	80	weaver
Watch	Samuel	m	70	weaver
Mason	Edmond	m	60	weaver
Duxbury	William	m	65	crofter
Roscow	Richard	m	80	ag labourer
Mather	Samuel	m	45	weaver
Hamer	Ann	f	55	no calling
Whitehead	Rachell	f	75	weaver
Godbert	James	m	40	weaver
Grundy	Thomas	m	70	weaver
Entwistle	Thomas	m	40	collier
Wylde	Mary	f	30	school mistress
Dobson	Easther	f	60	weaver
Hopenshaw	Mary	f	75	weaver
Whittle	Ellin	f	70	washerwoman
Russell	Ann	f	15	no calling
Kinder	Ellin	f	42	no calling
Gregory	Easther	f	25	weaver
Broomfield	Betty	f	40	weaver
Davis	Margret	f	15	no calling
Wainwright	Ann	f	25	weaver
Rothwell	Mary	f	25	no calling
Hingham	Betty	f	35	weaver
Partington	Ann	f	25	no calling
Mather	Ann	f	60	weaver
Barlow	Ann	f	35	weaver
Kay	Ruth	f	35	no calling
Entwistle	Beccy	f	65	collier
Ramell	Jane	f	60	no calling
Wainright	Thomas	m	1	no calling
Broomfield	John	m	10	no calling
Broomfield	William	m	5m	no calling
Hingham	William	m	8	no calling
Hingham	Ann	f	6	no calling
Hingham	James	m	3m	no calling
Hobson	John	m	10	no calling
Cowborn	John	m	8	no calling

The table lists 46 of 84 inmates in the census, all were born in Lancashire except Ellin Whittle.

1851 Census Return (partial) for Bolton Union Turton Workhouse

Surname	Christian Name	Sex	Rel	MS	Age	Occupation	Place of Birth
STAFF							
Lowe	Robert	m	head	m	50	workhouse master	Leyland
Lowe	Eliza	f	wife	m	52	workhouse matron	Leyland
INMATES							
Whiteley	Mary	f	none	u	60	seamstress	Great Bolton
Smith	David	m	none	w	82	cotton weaver	Ireland
Ellidge	Alice	f	none	u	47	cotton weaver	Great Bolton
Rogers	Joseph	m	none	u	7	scholar	Great Bolton
Grisdle	Joseph	m	none	u	26	cotton weaver	Great Bolton
Devenport	Mary	n	none	u	28	cotton rover	Great Bolton
Richardson	Eliza	f	none	u	24	none	Great Bolton
Ward	Mary	f	none	u	41	none	Lancs
Mangnall	James	m	none	u	23	none	Lancs
Turner	John	m	none	u	22	none	Lancs
Crowther	Catherine	f	none	w	78	house servant	Great Bolton
Baxter	Alice	f	none	u	20	house servant	Great Bolton
Grime	samuel	m	none		9	scholar	Great Bolton
Waddington	Alice	f	none	m	33	cotton piecer	Great Bolton
Waddington	Eliza	f	none		7	scholar	Great Bolton
Waddington	Sophia	f	none		5	none	Great Bolton
Taylor	Mary	f	none	m	30	cotton spinner	Wigan
Taylor	Edwin	m	none		2m		Great Bolton
Haslam	Ann	f	none	w	51	cotton weaver	Ireland
Shanoth	Alice	f	none	u	18	none	Turton
Morris	Amelia	f	none	u	45	none	Darcy Lever
Barlow	Joseph	m	none		11	scholar	Great Bolton
Fletcher	Alice	f	none	w	63	cotton weaver	Great Bolton
Fletcher	Jacob	m	none		13	none	Great Bolton
Sudworth	Mary	f	none	m	49	cotton weaver	Halliwell
Holt	Mary Ann	f	none		10	none	Great Bolton
Morrise	Ellen	f	none	w	73	cotton weaver	Wheelton
Smethurst	Betsy	f	none		11	scholar	Turton
Smethurst	Harriot	f	none		5	none	Turton
Smethurst	William	m	none		1		Turton
Makinson	Jane	f	none	u	45	none	Halliwell
Brindle	John	m	none	w	75	farm labourer	Tockholes
Fielding	Samuel	m	none	u	61	butcher	Turton deaf
Sharpies	Alice	f	none	u	65	cotton weaver	Lostock
Garnett	Christopher	m	none		10	scholar	Turton
Bury	Fanny	f	none	u	43	none	Worsley
Bury	Richard	m	none		2		Turton
Ashecroft	Meriam	f	none	u	54	house servant	Great Lever
Crook	Alice		none	w	61	cotton weaver	Westhoughton
Bury	Eliza		none	w	52	house servant	Rumworth
Holt	Thomas	m	none	w	77	house painter	Bradshaw
Entwisle	Ralph	m	none	u	57	cotton weaver	Entwisle
Rostron	Ellen	f	none	u	57	house servant	Entwisle
Riley	John	m	none	w	72	farm servant	Entwisle
Greenhalgh	Mary Ann	f	none	u	28	none	Harwood
Kay	Ruth	f	none	u	48	none	Harwood
Leach	Alice	f	none	u	37	none	Horwich

In the above table column headings Rel and MS refer to relationship to head of household and marital status respectively. The table includes 47 of the 76 inmates listed in the census.

1861 Census Return (partial) for the Bolton Union Turton Workhouse

Surname	Christian Name	Sex	MS	Age	Occupation	Birth Place
STAFF						
Taylor [Head]	John	m	m	45	master	Little Bolton
Taylor	Ellen	f	m	43	matron	Henley, Oxon
Whewell	Alice	f	w	45	general servant	Tyldesley
INMATES						
Kinkade	George	m		11	scholar	Great Bolton
Lyons	Jesse	m		11	scholar	Great Bolton
Taylor	William	m		8	scholar	Little Bolton
Smith	William	m		9	scholar	Great Bolton
MacDonald	Betty	f	w	71	housework	Ireland
Hargreaves	William	m		8	scholar	Great Bolton
Taylor	Thomas	m		9	scholar	Little Bolton
Eccles	Mary	f	w	70	housework	Great Bolton
Irving	John	m		12	scholar	Great Bolton
McLoughland	Francis	m		11	scholar	Great Bolton
McLoughland	James	m		12	scholar	Great Bolton
O'Hara	Charles	m		10	scholar	Liverpool
Bromily	John	m	w	70	factory worker	Great Bolton
Threfall	Mary Ann	f	w	52	housework	Great Bolton
O'Brien	Ellen	f	m	58	housework	Ireland
Maddin	William	m		12	scholar	Great Bolton
Boardman	William	m		8	scholar	Great Bolton
Boardman	Joseph	m		6	scholar	Great Bolton
McCann	Patrick	m		5	scholar	Great Bolton
McCann	John	m		7	scholar	Great Bolton
Horridge	Elizabeth	f	m	41	[illegible]	Whittle
Horridge	Edward	m		8	scholar	Great Bolton
Horridge	Henry	m		3		Great Bolton
Horridge	Susannah	f		4m		Great Bolton
Mulrooney	John	m		10	scholar	Great Bolton
Eyland	Ann	f	u	30	housework	Rochdale
Pilling	John	m	u	59	cotton weaver	Great Bolton
Berry	Jeremiah	m	u	43	sweep	Great Bolton
Morris	John	m		10	scholar	Great Bolton
Davis	Richard	m	w	51	machine maker	Great Bolton
Crompton	James	m		14	scholar	Great Bolton
Crompton	William	m		10	scholar	Little Bolton
Smith	Henry	m		14	scholar	Manchester
Smith	Nathan	m		10	scholar	Salford
Smith	Thomas	m	w	76	ag labourer	Little Bolton
Fletcher	Alice	f	w	72	cotton weaver	Little Bolton
Maddin	John	m		9	scholar	Little Bolton
Gerrard	William	m		11	scholar	Little Bolton
Linn	Samuel	m		11	scholar	Wigan
Sharratt	Alice	f		29	housework	Turton
Cunliffe	Margaret	f	w	62	hawker of fish	Ireland
Kenyon	Alice	f	w	64	housework	Little Bolton
Flitcroft	John	m		9	scholar	Great Bolton
Flitcroft	William	m		6	scholar	Great Bolton
Flitcroft	Thomas	m		5	scholar	Great Bolton
Garratt	Robert	m		11	occ scholar	Little Bolton
Garratt	John	m		7	scholar	Little Bolton

The above table includes 47 of the 101 inmates included in the census.

RULES,
TO BE OBSERVED IN THE
WORK-HOUSE,
AT TURTON.

ARTICLE FIRST

THAT the Master and Mistress be sober and orderly Persons, not given to Swear; and that they see the Orders strictly performed.

II.

THAT all Persons, upon their admission, deliver up what Household Goods and Cloaths they are possessed of, to the Master, in order to be cleaned and made useful for the Service of this House; and if any Person shall conceal any Linen, Woollen, or Household Furniture, with intent to Steal or Embezzle, such Persons shall immediately be carried before a Magistrate, in order to be imprisoned and punished with the utmost Rigour, as the Law Directs.

III.

THAT Prayers be read in the House every Evening before Supper; and that Grace be said before and after each Meal; and that all who are able, and do not attend at Prayers, shall lose their next Dinner.

IV.

THAT all that are able and in Health do go to Church every Sunday; Morning and Afternoon; that they return Home as soon as Divine Service is over; and if any be found loitering or begging by the Way, to lose their next Meal. And if at any time they get Drunk, or are guilty of prophane Cursing and Swearing, to be punished in the Stocks as the Law Directs, and to be debar'd going out during the Master's Pleasure.

V.

THAT no Person shall presume to go out of the Street Door without a Ticket of Leave, and to return in good order at the time appointed, upon Pain of being denied going out during the Master's Pleasure, and for the second Offence to be expelled the House.

VI.

THAT no distilled Liquor or strong Drink be brought into the House; and that whosoever shall disturb the House by brawling, quarreling, fighting, or abusive Language, shall lose one Day's Meat, and for the second Offence be put in the Dungeon twenty-four Hours.

VII.

THAT all Persons in health do rise in the Morning by five o'clock, and come to work by six, from Lady Day to Michaelmas; and from Michaelmas to Lady Day, that they rise by six, and come to work by seven, upon Pain of being kept on Bread and Water, or expelled the House.

VIII.

THAT all persons who through Idleness may pretend themselves sick, lame, or infirm, so as to be excused from their Labour, if such imposters be discovered by the Stomachs or by the Physicians, shall be carried before a Magistrate, to be punished severely as the Law Directs.

IX.

THAT they go to Bed in the Summer at nine, and in the Winter by eight o'Clock; and that the Master see all the Candles out.

X.

THAT all Provision be clean and well dressed; to go to Breakfast in the Summer at eight, and in the Winter at nine o'clock; Dinner at one all the Year; Supper at six; to be allowed Half an Hour at Breakfast, and a whole Hour at Dinner; and all that have not finished their Task by Supper, to work afterwards 'till finished; and great Care taken that they sit decently at Meat.

XI.

THAT if any Person falls Sick or Lame, Notice to be given to the Apothecary, by the Master, with all convenient speed to be taken Care of; and such other Victuals be allotted to the Patient besides what is daily used, as shall be thought proper by the Physician.

XII.

THAT all Beds be made in the Morning by nine, and every Room and Passage swept and cleaned by ten o'Clock, and to be washed three Times a Week in Summer, and once in Winter; the Dishes to be washed twice a Day or oftener; no waste Fire to be made, and in Summer none at all, except in the Kitchen or Wash-house in Time of Ironing.

XIII.

THAT all the Children be washed and cleaned by eight o'Clock in the Morning, and some proper Persons chose to teach them to Read.

XIV.

THAT the Nurse take care to make and mend all Linen and Cloaths, and when any Person dies, to deliver his other Cloaths to the Master, to be laid up in the Wardrobe or Store-room; and also every thing else they die possessed of, for the Use of the House.

XV.

THAT every Person endeavour to preserve Unity, and look upon themselves as one Family; and to prevent Disputes that may create Difference among themselves, by forging or telling Lies, such Persons so offending, on good Proof made thereof, shall be set upon a Stool, in the most public Place in the Dining-Room, whilst at Dinner, and a Paper prefixed upon his or her Breast, with these Words, (*Infamous Liar*) and likewise to lose that Meal.

XVI.

THAT the School-master or Mistress shall teach all the Children, as soon as they are fit to learn, the Church Catechism.

XVII.

THAT no Persons but a Benefactor to this House shall be allowed to come into any of the Wards, Dining-Room, or Working-Rooms, without Leave from the Governor; and if any desire to speak with any of the Poor, though their nearest Relations, they are not to be allowed without Leave.

XVIII.

THAT on the Lord's Day, either before Church or after Dinner, the Master do read, or cause to be read, the Psalms and Lessons appointed for the Morning Service; and after Evening Prayer, the Psalms and Lessons appointed for the Evening Service; and also a Section or Chapter out of the Whole Duty of Man.

XIX.

THAT the Vestry, every Month, or oftener if they see Cause, do examine all the Bills and accounts of the Expence of the maintaining the Poor in the Work-house; and also the accounts of all Materials brought in, or Work done or sold, and observe the several Rates and Prices charged, and give such Directions thereupon as they shall think fit, with regard to the better maintaining and employing the Poor, and saving the Parish Money.

XX.

THAT Care be taken none of the Materials of the several Manufactories be wasted or Spoiled, and that there be no defacing of Walls, or breaking of Windows; and that these Orders be publicly read every Week, that none may pretend Ignorance.

XXI.

THAT the Faults and Disorders of the Poor, whether old or young, who refuse or contemn the Reproofs of the Master or Mistress, or use ill Language against them, or neglect their Instructions, be recorded in a Book to be kept for that Purpose, and laid before the Directors or Overseers, that by their Authority and Admonition, Rudeness, Wickedness, and Dishonesty may be restrained, and Peace and good Order maintained; and that a Magistrate be solicited to punish all obstinate, perverse, and unruly Persons, according to their Crimes.

HAWORTH, PRINTER, BURY.

PUBLICATIONS OF TURTON LOCAL HISTORY SOCIETY

No 1	Stories of Turton Date Stones	R Lindop	1975
No 2	Lords of the Manor of Bradshaw	J J Francis	1977
No 3	Turton Tales (1)	R Lindop	1978
No 4	Bradshaw Works	J J Francis	1979
No 5	Bradshaw and Harwood Collieries	J J Francis	1982
No 6	The Bradshaw Flood (2nd Edition)	Rev S H Martin	1984
No 7	Enclosure of Edgworth Moor	J J Francis	1986
No 8	Turton Tales (2)	G Openshaw & J G Barber-Lomax	1987
No 9	Harwood Friendly Societies	J J Francis	1987
No 10	The Bradshaw Chapel History Trail	J J Francis	1988
No 11	The History of Turton Mill	R Lindop	1989
No 12	Datestones of Bradshaw & Harwood	AS & E Day	1989
No 13	The Enclosure of Harwood Commons	J J Francis	1990
No 14	Horrobin Mill	J J Francis	1992
No 15	Affetside: An Historical Survey	J J Francis	1994
No 16	Eagley Brook: A Lancashire Stream	Helen Heyes	1997
No 17	Harwood Vale: 1865-1965	J F Horridge	1997
No 18	Bradshaw Chapel I	J J Francis	1998
No 19	Bradshaw Chapel II	J J Francis	1998
No 20	2000 - Turton through the Ages	Ed. J F Horridge	1999
No 21	Quarlton	J J Francis	2000
No 21	Quarlton 2nd Edition	J J Francis	2009
No 22	Hardy Cornmill	J F Horridge	2001
No 23	People and Places of Turton	Ed. J F Horridge	2003
No 24	Lost Industries of Turton Moor	P M Harris	2003
No 25	Harwood Hill Farms & Riding Gate	J J Francis	2004
No 26	Samuel Scowcroft's Diary	Joan Francis	2005
No 27	Harwood - The Early Years	J F Horridge	2006
No 28	Birches	J J Francis & P M Harris	2006
No 29	Turton Fair	Alec Bagley & Pat Bagley	2007
No 30	Highways of Turton	J J Francis	2007
No 31	Churches and Chapels of Turton	D J Leeming	2008
No 32	The Barlow Institute 1909-2009	J J Francis	2009
No 33	Entwistle	C R Walsh	2011
No 34	Turton Workhouse	D J Leeming	2011
No 35	The Bradshaw Estate 1542-1919	J J Francis	2012
No 36	Mining in Turton	P M Harris	2013
No 37	Pubs in Turton Part 1	John Barlow	2018
No 38	Egerton	S J Tonge	2019

Printed in Great Britain
by Amazon